MULTIPLY YOUR SUCCESS WITH REAL ESTATE ASSISTANTS

Monica Reynolds

Real Estate
Education Company
a division of Dearborn Financial Publishing, Inc.

While a great deal of care has been taken to provide accurate and current information, the ideas, suggestions, general principles and conclusions presented in this text are subject to local, state and federal laws and regulations, court cases and any revisions of same. The reader is thus urged to consult legal counsel regarding any points of law—this publication should not be used as a substitute for competent legal advice.

Publisher: Kathleen A. Welton
Acquisitions Editor: Patrick J. Hogan
Associate Editor: Karen A. Christensen
Senior Project Editor: Jack L. Kiburz
Interior Design: Lucy Jenkins
Cover Design: Salvatore Concialdi

Printed in the United States of America

96   10   9   8   7   6   5

Library of Congress Cataloging-in-Publication Data

Reynolds, Monica.
    Multiply your success with real estate assistants : how to hire, train and manage your assistant : featuring 93 ready-to-use forms / by Monica Reynolds.
        p.   cm.
    Includes index.
    ISBN 0-7931-0776-8 (paper).
    1. Real estate agents—Training of—United States.   I. Title.
HD278.R52   1993
333.33′068′3—dc20
                                                        93-32671
                                                        CIP

Contents

Chapter 4. Effective Use of the Telephone   97

Chapter 5. Telemarketing   119

Chapter 6. The Importance of Checklists   149

List of Figures

Introduction: Should You Hire an Assistant?

Hiring an assistant will change more than just your income. Because real estate tends to spill over into other aspects of your life, having an assistant can affect almost everything—your moods, stress level, family life, as well as your ability to reach your goals. But although there are emotional aspects to hiring an assistant, you first must make sure it will be a good business decision.

No matter how many assistants you might have, you will still probably never get everything done that you want. But if you know you're not doing tasks that almost certainly would make money, then you should strongly consider hiring an assistant.

The priority of real estate agents is to be free to do what will produce income: working with buyers and sellers. Yet agents tend to be "control freaks"; they have to be the first and last person to touch everything. Usually it's sheer desperation to become more productive that drives them to give up some control.

I became an agent in 1979, and by 1984 I was a top producer in North Dakota with $3 million in sales and just a $65,000 average price. At the National Association of REALTORS® convention in New Orleans that year, some agents were talking about hiring assistants. It was a new concept, one that I wanted to implement immediately, because I was stuck and knew I could generate more sales volume. I had a burning desire to be number one.

My personal life at the time was even more challenging than my career. At age 34 my life underwent a radical change: My husband of 13 years and I had just completed our dream home. But before the mortgage was in place, he decided our marriage was over and I was left with three small children. Could I handle the financial challenge of qualifying for a mortgage and then make the payments? I had to give it a try.

To maintain our lifestyle, I had to double my income. How was I to do this? I needed to double myself, and so I hired my first assistant within one week of returning to Fargo from the NAR convention. It was an intense and exciting time. I found Jane Ferguson, who was a past client, the sister of my best friend and a single mom looking for a flexible job.

Our first day together was challenging. I had never been a boss before, and not knowing what else to do, I introduced Jane to everyone in the office, showed her my desk and the ladies room, introduced her to the broker and then took her to lunch. Day two I sent her to the grocery store, had her drop off paperwork at the lender and she answered three phone calls.

Over the next few days, however, I tried to shift some responsibilities to her. I knew that I only wanted to speak with buyers, sellers, contractors and anyone else who could help me generate a sale. It turned out that Jane was very organized. Almost by accident we started to develop checklists, systems, phone-calling procedures and accountability charts. She ordered her own cards and had her picture taken for my new brochure that would show clients she was part of a team working to help them reach their goals. Along the way we learned a lot. If only I had a road map in the beginning!

You'll find this book to be the kind of guide that will get you where you want to go. You'll go step-by-step from deciding whether you need an assistant to ensuring that he or she makes you more profitable.

This book can take years off your learning curve and save you thousands of dollars in costly mistakes. Much of what I've learned has been reduced to easy-to-use forms and checklists that we've developed over the years. They should be invaluable in hiring and training an assistant who can further your real estate career.

Many top producers I talk with know that the way to increase business is through the effective use of an assistant. Here's what Terry Paranych of RE/MAX Edmonton, Alberta, Canada, says: "Our newly implemented Sanford systems are awesome. We've listed three homes, of which two are now pending—*all in one week!* And that's because we've modeled your systems. We know this will only get better!"

ARE YOU READY TO MULTIPLY YOUR SUCCESS?

An assistant is the only way you can multiply your production. But how can you be sure it's the best answer for you? This book will go over the many tasks an assistant can do for you. If you're feeling overwhelmed, exhausted or frustrated with your business, you'll probably find your answer here. I've developed a simple test you can take (Figure I.1 on page xvi) to determine if you're ready for this step.

Back in 1984, when I was considering hiring an assistant for the first time, I would have answered yes to every one of these questions. As I drove through town, I saw my competitors' signs on the front lawns of houses that should have been my listings. My son was disappointed that I was not able to attend his hockey games. I needed a vacation. Worst of all, I was beginning to hate real estate—a very bad sign, because to achieve great success you must love what you do.

Real estate agents often ask me how much they need to earn to make it worthwhile to hire an assistant. Typically, successful agents will reach a production plateau that they just can't seem to break. After all, the best way to increase your income is to contact prospects, but there is only so much one person can do. With the help of an assistant, you can double your efforts, double your income and double your free time. If you see yourself at that plateau and you want to do better, it's time to hire an assistant. My comfort zone was between $2 million and $3 million. Your comfort zone, of course, will depend partly on the value of homes in your area.

I have provided prospecting tools in this book, because that is how assistants can become income generators and "pay their way." In a sense, the key issue in deciding on hiring an assistant is not how much you earn but rather how much you *could* earn. My wake-up call was those competitors' signs. Don't consider only financial issues, either. We all know how real estate can take over our personal lives. If you are enjoying financial success but feel you are neglecting other aspects of your life, perhaps an assistant is the answer. Consider the benefit of more free time as your income goes up.

SHOULD YOU HIRE A LICENSED ASSISTANT?

This is the most-asked question in my seminars: "Should my assistant be licensed or unlicensed?" The answer to that question is based on your needs and market area.

The Sanford Group does not employ licensed assistants because we don't need them. There are several reasons for this. The main reason is that we refuse to train the competition. Many times an applicant will tell me that he or she wishes to become a REALTOR® to model Walter Sanford's success, to work for him and learn from him. This is not at all the type of assistant I am looking for as a team player. The other reason has to do with money. It is expensive licensing an assistant and keeping up with the educational requirements, brokerage fees, licensing fees and time out of the office.

Recently, I was asked to speak before a California Association of REALTORS® task force formulated to address the issue of unlicensed assistants. Following are some of the conclusions:

- An unlicensed assistant may not negotiate, write or amend contracts.
- An unlicensed assistant may not speak of price, terms or condition of a property to a client or potential client.
- An unlicensed assistant may not solicit for the sole purpose of engaging an appointment for the agent to write a contract regarding the sale or purchase of the property.
- An unlicensed assistant may not discuss financing avenues with any client.

Many states require that assistants be licensed. Sometimes the broker you affiliate with requires that your assistant be licensed because it's office policy, or for legal reasons. Sometimes agents who travel choose to have a licensed assistant to help with buyers and to take care of business in their absence.

There are many pluses to having a licensed assistant work for you. This person can become an extension of your efforts, and you don't have to worry about limiting his or her responsibilities.

Contact the Department of Real Estate in your state and ask for guidelines. It is also important to see if your local Board of REALTORS® has any specific requirements. Another step in this process is to check with your office and, of course, the broker. After you have all the information, then you can determine, based on the needs you have formulated, whether you need a licensed or unlicensed assistant.

PAYROLL

I am often asked to discuss the issue of "employee versus independent contractor." I am a firm believer in hiring an employee. It is just not worth it legally to do it any other way. Plus, the paperwork that is necessary when hiring an independent contractor can be an incredible endeavor.

Consider using a payroll company to prepare checks and statements. There are many such companies to choose from in your market. A bookkeeper would also be able to provide these services. Our particular service will calculate all payroll checks, figure payroll taxes and deposit them, prepare and file payroll tax returns, give us management reports, handle workers' compensation deductions and reconcile our payroll account. The cost can be incredibly low compared to the time it would take you to figure it all out.

Another possibility to help you run this part of your business is to check with your bank. The banks in our area are soliciting this type of business.

Whomever you choose, make sure they have the resources and experience to deliver the services you need.

WALTER SANFORD'S SYSTEMS

The information and tools in this book will help you reach your full potential. The forms, letters, systems, checklists and scripts have been collectively formulated by Walter Sanford and myself. Walter Sanford of Sanford Group, Inc., Long Beach, California, is recognized as one of the top REALTORS® in North America. Walter is known as a real estate systems genius, which is the reason for his incredible real estate production. The value of this book is that it provides the basics of a system with proven results.

As you read, you will have to make adjustments on the various forms and checklists for your particular market and methods. Every market has different requirements. This information is a foundation or "map" from which you can design your own checklists and systems pertinent to your market needs. We at the Sanford Group wish you the best of success as you develop your own systems and reach for higher goals.

FIGURE I.1

Test Your Needs

1. Are you frustrated trying to break into another income bracket?

2. Are you missing transactions because you don't always get back to people in a timely manner?

3. Do the little details that don't make you any money prevent you from prospecting?

4. Is your production level at least $2 million to $3 million?

5. Does your family complain about your absences?

6. Do you need more help with prospecting?

7. Do you need a vacation?

8. Do you sometimes think you want to get out of the real estate business?

9. Do you want more money?

10. Do you need more time in the day?

11. Do you still like your career?

12. Are you goal-oriented?

Six Steps To Finding the Right Assistant

After deciding that you need to hire an assistant, how do you go about it? Working for a superstar agent—the kind most likely to hire an assistant—isn't easy. You want someone who is willing to work hard, show initiative and stay calm in all situations. Such people are not always simple to find. What's more, you often won't be totally sure whether you've made a good choice until weeks or months after hiring someone.

Before starting the interview process, determine the most important characteristics you'll need in a person. Knowing this will help you decide where and how to look for an assistant. For instance, are phone skills essential or would you prefer someone who will concentrate on keeping files in order? Do you need a person to work closely with lenders and title companies? If so, try to find someone with a real estate background. It's possible to discover agents who would rather help another agent and draw a paycheck than rely on commissions.

If you prefer to train someone to follow your own system, a college student with little experience could be the right choice. Obviously, you'll adjust your marketing based on these decisions. Soon you will see the variety of backgrounds that people can offer. One might be experienced on the telephone and with customer service. Another might have worked at an escrow company. Both would have appealing backgrounds, but for different reasons.

Because you don't know what the next person has to offer, promise yourself not to hire the first applicant who comes through your door. What you might call "intuition" may in fact be just impatience. While you want to get the hiring over with and return to work, you'll lose time and money over the long run by being hasty now. Plan on spending two weeks to find the right assistant. It's worth the effort—after all, you might end up spending more time with your assistant than you do with your family!

A combination of skill, experience and the proper attitude is necessary in a useful real estate assistant. To find one, you'll need to be able to spot these essential elements. In this chapter we'll give you the tools to do so.

STEP ONE: WRITING THE JOB DESCRIPTION (FIGURE 1.1)

The first step in hiring your assistant is to write a job description. This task forces you to think about how you will use the assistant and what you expect from this person. You will never find the right person for the job until you have a clear idea of what is "right." Writing a job description will help you develop your interview questions and make you better able to answer applicants' questions about the details of the position.

Figure 1.1 is a generic sample job description. Throughout this book, you'll see lots of ideas for how an assistant can boost your production. I urge you to go through the book and write a job description of your own. Chapter 3 includes a specific job description for our administrative assistant. By making the job description specific and goal-oriented, you can lay the groundwork for a productive relationship on your assistant's first day on the job.

STEP TWO: THE AD (FIGURE 1.2)

I wrote this ad with the help of our advertising agent, Norm Robinson, of Fargo, North Dakota. When Walter and I had ultimately decided we needed to hire another person to handle our systems newsletter, we groaned in unison at the thought of the hiring process. Then Norm showed us an effective ad he had developed that would guarantee a flood of responses. Great! The more selection, the better the final choice. We took the basic concept of Norm's ad and tailored it to the needs of our real estate office—and it was pure MAGIC! I promise you will be inundated with résumés. People like to respond to this ad whether they are currently employed or not. Here are a couple of quotes from agents who have used it:

> When I placed that ad in my local paper, I received over 85 responses. It was incredible to have that many responses when before I normally would receive only about three to five inquiries.
> —Erica West, RE/MAX, Fountain Hills, Arizona

> This is the greatest ad written! It really enhanced the quality of the applicants and saved us hiring time.
> —Doug and Marie Drummond, Prudential California Realty, La Canada, California

The quality of people who responded to this ad was outstanding. What a great surprise to have over 100 responses to the ad I placed and a great selection of potential assistants. Thanks for your ad—it is absolutely the best.

—Rich Toepper, RE/MAX Tradition, Woodstock, Illinois

Six Tips for Placing Your Ad (Figure 1.3)

Remember, even though this is a successful ad and the response is overwhelming, don't forget about networking. Consider your business and personal spheres of influence to search for the perfect assistant. Two assistants who were absolutely terrific came from totally unrelated sources. One assistant I hired was a previous client, and another was a telephone receptionist at a car dealership.

Walter is constantly looking at title and escrow companies for people who impress him with their attitude and customer service skills. We then call them and ask if they would be interested in applying for an assistant job. This ad can be a great source, but never neglect thinking of people who have already proved to you that they are effective and have good interpersonal skills. They have the advantage of being familiar with the business, with established relationships, and they could be a great asset to you.

STEP THREE: REVIEWING RÉSUMÉS (FIGURE 1.4)

Allow at least a week to collect all résumés before you start the interview process. This is critical, because often it seems that the late response is a great applicant. When the résumés start arriving, put them in a file on your desk. When you have finished collecting them, you can review all of them at the same time.

I place all the résumés on our conference table and look at each one individually and carefully. I can eliminate some even before reading. Those that are not neat in appearance or are done haphazardly are eliminated. I've had résumés submitted on the back of children's schoolwork. I even had someone call to tell me her résumé was done and I could come and pick it up. Yikes! Who would be working for whom in that case?

Expect to receive at least 30 résumés. For the first cut, I recommend that you narrow the applicants you will consider to 10. The 10 best applicants are all you need to spend time interviewing. Whether you received 30 or 130, this is a good rule to follow.

Once you have made your selection, call the top applicants and set up interviews at your office.

What about the stack of résumés you have eliminated? A return call is important, not only because it is a courtesy, but also because you always want to have the most professional appearance possible in the community. One of the applicants you reject may become a future business lead. For example, one applicant I chose not to interview called me later when her husband was transferred and asked me to sell their condo. Even though I hadn't even interviewed her, she remembered the contact with our office as a good experience. Don't spend too much time on this, though. If they aren't home, just leave the message on an answering machine (if they have one), unless the applicant is already a business contact. In that case, you may want to use your call as an opportunity to maintain the relationship.

Another possibility is to write a small note to each applicant. If you don't let them know quickly that the position is filled, your phone will start ringing. We have a letter in our computer that we send out as soon as we make the decision.

STEP FOUR: INTERVIEW 1 (FIGURE 1.5–FIGURE 1.6)

I recommend scheduling interviews in 30-minute slots. You don't need more time than that. Keep in mind that these are merely initial interviews so that you can meet the applicants in person. This is your opportunity to have a conversation with them and start to form an opinion. You are still gathering information and not making decisions at this point. Have them complete the application (Figure 1.5) prior to the interview.

In Figure 1.6 are 34 questions I believe are important to ask each applicant. Notice that these are open-ended questions designed to create a dialogue. The individual in front of you may become the person you spend more hours in the day with than your family. Of course, ask the obvious—how long they've lived in the area, where they went to high school. These kinds of rapport-building questions are important, but not as important as the questions in Figure 1.6.

As you can probably determine by reading the questions, you'll get some interesting answers. Every answer gives you a bit more insight into the personality and attitudes of the applicant. After all, the person who's going to be your assistant must be the right match for your personality, working style and the marketplace you serve.

One applicant told me that in her spare time she worked on and rode Harley-Davidson motorcycles. I found that interesting and thought nothing more of it until she pushed up her sleeves and displayed two scorpion tattoos. Based upon my clientele, I decided that "Ray and Jake" (the two scorpions) were not really the image I was after.

Another applicant told me that working under a lot of stress really annoyed her. Her previous employer was always in a hurry, yelling for misplaced files, looking for his car keys, asking the same question four times in a row, constantly distracted, forgetful and sometimes rude. Well, she had just described

Walter Sanford. You may be smiling right now, because she probably described you, too. She was not considered for the position.

The Rating Sheet (Figure 1.7)

This rating sheet should be completed after your first interview to record the impressions you had of each applicant. At the end of Interview 1, thank applicants for their time and tell them you will contact them within a week with your decision. *Golden Rule:* Do not hire the first applicant who appears to have all the right answers. The last applicant you interview may be the one most qualified for the position. And never hire anyone on the spot. Let yourself digest and evaluate all the information you have gathered before taking action. In fact, it may be a good idea to sleep on it before going through the second round of cuts.

After interviewing all ten applicants, try to narrow your choices to five, or, even better, to three if you can. If you are finding it hard to decide, take a minute to imagine the person working in your office every day. Was there anything that bothered you about the applicant? Anything that made you feel uncomfortable? Would this person be someone you would want to see on a bad day? Did you communicate easily with her or him? Remember, the best assistant for you will be someone who is easy to work with. You don't need to add a relationship that takes a lot of work to your workday.

When you have completed your second round of eliminations, call your top choices and schedule Interview 2. Then call or send a letter to the Interview 1 applicants you do not wish to consider for the position, thanking them for their time.

STEP FIVE: INTERVIEW 2 (FIGURE 1.8)

Now you are ready to proceed to the next step in the process that will help you find the best assistant. This is the fun part! Allow yourself a little more time than you did with the first interview, because you want to have enough information at the end of the second round of interviews to make a final decision. Interview 2 gives you the chance to take a second look at your top applicants and to ask ten additional questions that are more probing.

Once these ten questions are answered, you should be able to determine if the person is someone you would like to add to your team. If the interview went well and you felt the applicant definitely had the attitude you were looking for, then it is time to test his or her skills.

Characteristics for Walter's Team (Figure 1.9)

Here's a list of qualities that are important for success as a real estate assistant.

STEP SIX: SKILLS TESTS (FIGURES 1.10–1.18)

It is imperative to test the skills of an applicant you are seriously considering. This was one of my biggest errors in my early years of interviewing applicants, and it is something that people often overlook. It is a tempting shortcut, but you cannot assume anything, even from people who are impressive in conversation and have impeccable résumés. Skipping this step can result in making the wrong choice and hiring someone who can't do the work—a costly mistake that may put you in the uncomfortable position not only of having to fire someone but also of having to begin the entire interview process again. Good applicants don't remain unemployed for long, and by the time you are rid of your bad hire, all of your top applicants may have found jobs.

Eight Skills You Can Test in Less Than 30 Minutes

1. Computer—To test applicants' skills, have them go over to the computer and show you what they can do. If they appear lost, they probably will stay lost. If the skills are there, they will be comfortable immediately—or, if the system is new to them, they will ask appropriate questions to be able to do basic functions. Sometimes we send the new assistant to our computer consultant for a two-day orientation on our systems. Letting the experts instruct in that area can save time and avoid interrupting the normal work flow.

2. Typing—If applicants claim to be able to type 45 wpm or faster, definitely have them demonstrate this skill. Take them over to the typewriter or computer, hand them a letter right off the top of your desk and have them type it. It's a simple test. Amazingly, I have had applicants handle the two interviews magnificently and then spend 45 minutes typing one short letter. I also have had applicants say they would come back "tomorrow" with their glasses to take the test. They never returned.

3. Basic Skills Quiz (Figures 1.10 and 1.11)—This simple test verifies some basic but important skills an assistant should have.

4. Spelling (Figures 1.12 and 1.13)—Though many offices have a "spell check" feature on their systems, it's still nice to know that the applicant has spelling skills.

5. Math (Figures 1.14 and 1.15)—We ask five math questions. It's obviously important that assistants dealing in financial transactions have basic math skills.

6. Letters: Punctuation, Salutations and Writing—Ask applicants to address and properly punctuate a standard letter. You shouldn't have to teach an assistant basic grammar skills or the proper way to format a letter. You can also check basic writing skills by describing a simple scenario and asking the applicant to prepare a letter for you.

   Example: Please type a letter to John Smith thanking him for the referral. Tell him it was great to see him at lunch Tuesday and that I'll call him next week.

7. Proofreading (Figures 1.16 and 1.17)—Retype a letter you received, but include numerous misspelled words and typos. Give it to applicants to correct. An assistant who misspells words or uses them improperly can damage your professional image. For example, Walter received a letter from the president of a mortgage lending company stating, "It was great to here from you." There's a mistake that spell check won't catch.

8. Problem Solving/Prioritizing (Figure 1.18)—The following problems will help you determine applicants' problem-solving skills. The ability to prioritize problems and daily duties are a great skill.

The Perfect Assistant (Figure 1.19)

When you are ready to make your final decision, review this profile for some helpful hints.

FIGURE 1.1

Job Description: Assistant

Goals

To help the agent increase business
To help the agent decrease expenses
To assist the agent in developing clients for life

Responsibilities

Monitors and follows up on all listings
Monitors and follows up on all sales in process/escrows
Maintains business supply inventory
Handles all incoming phone calls
Returns all phone calls in a timely manner
Handles all checking accounts, deposits and reconciliations
Sends out expired-listing letters daily
Sends out FSBO letters weekly
Sends out People Farm area mailings quarterly
Calls past clients one hour a day for leads
Fills out update reports daily
Communicates with agent daily
Informs office of new listings and sales
Develops flyers for new listings
Posts all new listings on office board
Posts all new sales on office board
Monitors weekly, monthly and yearly goals
Keeps all files neat and orderly
Keeps and organizes all property keys
Goes to closings and brings the "move-in box"
Updates all client records in computer
Is responsible for all data entry and reports
Is responsible for all correspondence
Asks personal people farm for referrals for the agent

FIGURE 1.2

Sample Advertisement

EXECUTIVE'S ASSISTANT

Immediate opening for assistant to assist
real estate executive. You should be an
organizer, a positive person, a good communicator
—both written and verbal—experienced with
computer/word processing, have a good
sense of humor, be a fast learner with a quick
mind and be willing to work hard and smart.
You'll work in a fast-paced real estate
office in Long Beach. We offer an exciting
atmosphere in a people-oriented business. This
is NOT an entry-level position. Please
indicate salary desired. The first step is to
send or deliver your resume to:

SANFORD GROUP, INC.
3700 E. 7th Street
Long Beach, CA 90804

Fax: 310-434-6353

FIGURE 1.3

Six Tips for Placing Your Ad

1. Placing this ad in a local community paper offers a lot less expense and more visibility than your area's larger newspaper.

2. When using larger newspapers, such as the *Los Angeles Times,* you need to reduce the ad. This would be very expensive to place in its entirety.

3. Do not put your phone number on the ad. You want the written résumés delivered or faxed to you. I repeat, do not put your phone number on the ad. You do not want to speak with all of the people who respond to the ad. It can be a real time-waster.

4. Always ask the applicant to indicate salary level. This will allow you to eliminate someone who wants to start at $100,000. Believe me, I have had out-of-work executives, especially in the California market, applying for the job.

5. Put the ad in your local REALTOR® news or MLS book.

6. Fax the ad to local colleges. It also works great for a part-time position. Once I was lucky enough to have one of the clerical administrators at a college see the ad and apply for the job. I hired her and she was terrific. Remember, colleges have skilled personnel sitting at desks who might want a career change.

FIGURE 1.4

Eight Tips for Reading a Résumé

When I start the process of elimination, I look for these items in the résumés:

1. *Consistent job flow*—You don't want a "job jumper" who has a job change every six months or less.

2. *Customer service background*—You want someone with good people skills and experience.

3. *Real estate background*—Someone already familiar with the industry brings with them a knowledge of the business, and that can save you some training time.

4. *Educational background*—This can give you an idea of the applicant's motivation for self-advancement, although it should not be the only consideration.

5. *Specific job skills and training* (computer, typing, dictation)—A variety of skills can indicate that an applicant is easy to cross-train and can pick up new skills readily.

6. *Recommendation letter from a previous employer*—This can be a big plus, since someone who hired the applicant is evaluating his or her work for you.

7. *Professional presentation*—Look for well-written sentences, no typos, and correct punctuation. General appearance of the résumé is very important, because it shows you what the applicant considers to be a final written product. Remember, your assistant will be preparing written materials for you that reflect on your professionalism, and if he or she already knows what is appropriate, you are on the same track from day one.

8. *Something that makes you want to meet and personally interview the applicant*—This can be an overall impression or a specific item, but if you don't want to know more about the applicant after reading the résumé, don't waste your time on an interview.

FIGURE 1.5

Real Estate Assistant Job Application

Date: _____

```
Name: _____

Present Address: _____

_____

Permanent Address: _____

_____

Phone Number: _____

Social Security Number: _____
```

State name/relationship of any relatives in our employ:

_____ Referred by _____

_____

Employment

Are you currently employed?   YES   NO

If so, where? _____

May we contact your employer?   YES   NO

Please list your last four (4) employers, starting with the present, and include job and reason for leaving.

1. _____
   (Place of employment)   (Salary)

   Date (month/year) of employment: _____ to _____

   Reason for leaving: _____

   _____

FIGURE 1.5 (Continued)

2. _____
   (Place of employment)   (Salary)

   Date (month/year) of employment: _____ to _____

   Reason for leaving: _____

   _____

3. _____
   (Place of employment)   (Salary)

   Date (month/year) of employment: _____ to _____

   Reason for leaving: _____

   _____

4. _____
   (Place of employment)   (Salary)

   Date (month/year) of employment: _____ to _____

   Reason for leaving: _____

   _____

References

1. Name: _____

   Address: _____

   Phone: _____

2. Name: _____

   Address: _____

   Phone: _____

3. Name: _____

   Address: _____

   Phone: _____

FIGURE 1.5 (Continued)

4. Name: _____

    Address: _____

    Phone: _____

In case of emergency, notify: _____

_____

I authorize investigation of all statements in this application and I understand that misrepresentation or omission is reason for dismissal. I understand that my employment is for no definite period and may be terminated at any time.

Signed: _____

Date: _____

FIGURE 1.6

Thirty-four Interview Questions

1. Why are you considering giving up your current job or position?

2. What exactly did you do at your last job? Tell me what your average workday was like and what you were responsible for handling.

3. What accomplishments are you most proud of professionally? Personally?

4. If you had more spare time, what would you do with it?

5. How would you handle a customer who called and was angry?

6. How would you handle a customer who was upset about something the agent hadn't delivered? Could you turn that situation around and make that person a happy client?

7. Do you tend to dig into the tough problems in the morning, afternoon or late in the day?

8. Why do you do the tough stuff at that time?

9. How many tasks can you handle at once?

10. How do you organize your work?

11. What kind of people annoy you?

12. Tell me about the worst supervisor you ever worked for.

13. Tell me how you handled working in that situation.

14. What decisions did you make at your last job and how did you go about making those decisions?

15. Have you had problems working with others?

16. What experience have you had in real estate? Have you ever purchased or sold a home or handled rentals?

FIGURE 1.6 (Continued)

17. What aspects of working in a real estate office interest you?

18. What do you hope to be doing two years from now? How much do you want to be earning?

19. Tell me about your biggest frustrations in your business/working career.

20. What has been your most rewarding work-related experience?

21. What are your career goals? (Are they serious, well-thought-out goals, coinciding with this position?)

22. If anything would take you away from working, what would it be? (Kids, smoke break, etc.)

23. Do you have reliable transportation?

24. Do you listen to tapes? Have you heard of Walter Sanford, Brian Tracy, Zig Ziglar? Have you attended any seminars?

25. How fast can you type? May I test you?

26. What computer skills do you have, specifically DOS and word processing?

27. Have you driven around Long Beach? Can you find specific neighborhoods?

28. Have you ever been a real estate agent?

29. Have you worked in escrow?

30. Have you taken any courses regarding title insurance or worked in title insurance?

31. Have you taken any time management courses?

32. Do you use a daily planner of any type?

33. Have you had extensive experience with over-the-phone client service? What was it?

34. What does a "client for life" mean to you?

FIGURE 1.7

Rating Sheet

Name of Prospective Employee: _____

Date of Interview: _____

Appearance	1	2	3	4	5
Positive attitude	1	2	3	4	5
Poise	1	2	3	4	5
Voice	1	2	3	4	5
Optimistic, fun, zip	1	2	3	4	5
Quick to learn	1	2	3	4	5
Can prioritize well	1	2	3	4	5
Self-starter	1	2	3	4	5
"Can-do" attitude	1	2	3	4	5
Can deal with difficult people	1	2	3	4	5
Team player	1	2	3	4	5
Open to criticism	1	2	3	4	5
Problem solver	1	2	3	4	5
Mature	1	2	3	4	5
Dependable	1	2	3	4	5
Focused	1	2	3	4	5
Willing to make decisions	1	2	3	4	5
Good telephone voice	1	2	3	4	5
Could handle difficult customers diplomatically and effectively on the phone	1	2	3	4	5
Good penmanship	1	2	3	4	5
Typing skills	1	2	3	4	5
Computer skills, DOS/IBM	1	2	3	4	5
Knows Long Beach areas very well	1	2	3	4	5

FIGURE 1.7 (Continued)

General Comments: _____

_____

_____

_____

_____

_____

_____

_____

_____

_____

FIGURE 1.8

Ten Questions for the
Second Interview

1. Where do you hope to be in five years?

2. What do you think it takes to be a successful real estate agent? Have you personally ever worked with an agent?

3. Describe the time you were most motivated at any of your previous jobs.

4. When were you least motivated?

5. How do you schedule your time?

6. How do you set priorities and solve problems of conflicting priorities?

7. How long would you be interested in holding a position such as this?

8. What is your greatest strength?

9. What would you consider to be your greatest weakness?

10. Describe the worst day on your last job. How did you handle it?

FIGURE 1.9

Walter's Team

These are the qualities we look for in each of our staff:

- Able to communicate professionally, both written and verbal

- Enjoys a busy pace and handles stress well

- Can prioritize work—is organized and can set weekly goals and stick to them

- Can set daily schedule and stick to it

- Is dedicated and can observe confidentiality

- Is a self-starter, highly motivated, enthusiastic and a take-charge person

- Has excellent typing skills and is computer literate

- Has good poise and people skills and is not easily intimidated

- Is happy, with a positive attitude and a good sense of humor

- Is a fast learner with a quick mind, and is willing to work hard and smart

- Is brutally honest and loyal

FIGURE 1.10

Basic Skills Quiz

Please read the directions and complete each section as indicated.

Capitalization:

Circle each letter or word that you feel should be capitalized.

mr. jones	united kingdom	helen thomas
the midwest	navy blue	north dakota
chicago	gulf of mexico	vaseline
economics	aunt sophie	economics 101
the sun rises in the east		
the saturday evening post (magazine)		

Salutations:

Please provide the correct salutations for a business letter.

Example: James Monroe   *Salutation:* Dear Mr. Monroe:

Mr. Leo Lion and   *Salutation:*
    Mr. Thomas Caton

Susan Smith   *Salutation:*

Mr. Steve Hawkins and   *Salutation:*
    Ms. Maria Nelson

Mr. and Mrs. Scott Smith   *Salutation:*

Helen Brown, M.D.   *Salutation:*

Dr. Gerald Thomas   *Salutation:*

Dr. Lloyd Smith and   *Salutation:*
    his wife, Mary

The wife of Dr. Irving Zack   *Salutation:*

FIGURE 1.11

Answers to Basic Skills Quiz

(We have made the necessary corrections for you.)

Capitalization:

Circle each letter or word that you feel should be capitalized.

Mr. Jones	United Kingdom	Helen Thomas
The Midwest	navy blue	North Dakota
Chicago	Gulf of Mexico	Vaseline
economics	Aunt Sophie	Economics 101

The sun rises in the east

The Saturday Evening Post (magazine)

Salutations:

Please provide the correct salutations for a business letter.

Example: James Monroe	*Salutation:* Dear Mr. Monroe:
Mr. Leo Lion and Mr. Thomas Caton	*Salutation:* Dear Mr. Lion and Mr. Caton:
Susan Smith	*Salutation:* Dear Ms. Smith:
Mr. Steve Hawkins and Ms. Maria Nelson	*Salutation:* Dear Mr. Hawkins and Ms. Nelson:
Mr. and Mrs. Scott Smith	*Salutation:* Dear Mr. and Mrs. Smith:
Helen Brown, M.D.	*Salutation:* Dear Dr. Brown:
Dr. Gerald Thomas	*Salutation:* Dear Dr. Thomas:
Dr. Lloyd Smith and his wife, Mary	*Salutation:* Dear Dr. and Mrs. Smith:
The wife of Dr. Irving Zack	*Salutation:* Dear Mrs. Zack:

FIGURE 1.12

Spelling Test

Circle the words that are misspelled.

absence	eminant	mispelled	sieze
analasis	extrememly	ommision	seperate
bookeeper	flexible	persistant	tangable
changeble	guarantee	practically	temperary
competant	illegall	rational	until
decision	leisur	recommend	vicious
defer	miscellaneus		

Alphabetizing

1. Please alphabetize this list.

    1. McLaughlin   1.
    2. Meier   2.
    3. Morgan   3.
    4. MacDonald   4.
    5. Miller   5.

2. Please alphabetize this list.

    1. Yaeger   1.
    2. Boeder   2.
    3. Girelle   3.
    4. Johnson   4.
    5. Kline   5.
    6. Wilson   6.
    7. Thomas   7.
    8. Egert   8.
    9. Nixon   9.
    10. Reynolds   10.

FIGURE 1.13

Answers to Spelling Test

(We have corrected each word and have placed an asterisk (*) next to the incorrect words.)

absence	*eminent	*misspelled	*seize
*analysis	*extremely	*omission	*separate
*bookkeeper	flexible	*persistent	*tangible
*changeable	guarantee	practically	*temporary
*competent	*illegal	rational	until
decision	*leisure	recommend	vicious
defer	*miscellaneous		

Answers to Alphabetizing

1. Please alphabetize this list.

1.	McLaughlin	1.	MacDonald
2.	Meier	2.	McLaughlin
3.	Morgan	3.	Meier
4.	MacDonald	4.	Miller
5.	Miller	5.	Morgan

2. Please alphabetize this list.

1.	Yaeger	1.	Boeder
2.	Boeder	2.	Egert
3.	Girelle	3.	Girelle
4.	Johnson	4.	Johnson
5.	Kline	5.	Kline
6.	Wilson	6.	Nixon
7.	Thomas	7.	Reynolds
8.	Egert	8.	Thomas
9.	Nixon	9.	Wilson
10.	Reynolds	10.	Yaeger

FIGURE 1.14

Math Test

1. Walter just sold a house for $329,000. He was paid a 7 percent commission. What was the amount of his commission?

    Answer: _____

2. Walter just listed an apartment building for $3.7 million. Please write that numerically.

    Answer: _____

3. Please add these figures: $4.17, $1,322.91, $482.29, $615.01, $22,400.89.

    Answer: _____

4. Please subtract $89.03 and $134.26 from the answer to #3.

    Answer: _____

5. What is:
    A) 92 ÷ 6,   B) 172 ÷ 11,   C) 19 ÷ 182?

    A) _____ **B)** _____ **C)** _____

FIGURE 1.15

Answers to Math Test

1. Walter just sold a house for $329,000. He was paid a 7 percent commission. What was the amount of his commission?

   Answer: $23,030.00

2. Walter just listed an apartment building for $3.7 million. Please write that numerically.

   Answer: $3,700,000.00

3. Please add these figures: $4.17, $1,322.91, $482.29, $615.01, $22,400.89.

   Answer: $24,825.27

4. Please subtract $89.03 and $134.26 from the answer to #3.

   Answer: $24,601.98

5. What is: A) 92 ÷ 6,   B) 172 ÷ 11,   C) 19 ÷ 182?

   A) 15.33   **B)** 15.64   **C)** $.104

FIGURE 1.16

Proofreading Test

January 10, 1994

Mr. Mike jones
    234 Apple way
Long Beach, Ca 90807

Dear Mr. Jones,

Enclosed is your closing statement for this past yera. I am sure, in all of the confusion of a real estate transaction, this paperwork is not easily accessible. I thought I would help by providing yu with this document.

As you know,this will be one of the first documents that your accountant ask for.By providing you with this serviec, I hop I am releiving one of the small details that seems so plentiful during tax time.

Please have yuou accountant call me if he or she has any questions. Inn addition, if I can offer any further assistance, perwork, or real estate advisee, please don't hesitate to call.

It is my goal to have you and your family as client for life.

sincerely,

Walter S. Sanford
PRESIDENT SGI

WSS/mer

FIGURE 1.17

Corrected Proofreading Test

January 10, 1994

Mr. Mike *jones
*   234 Apple *way
Long Beach, Ca* 90807

Dear Mr. Jones,*

Enclosed is your closing statement for this past *yera. I am sure, in all of the confusion of a real estate transaction, this paperwork is not easily accessible. I thought I would help by providing *yu with this document.

As you know,*this will be one of the first documents that your accountant *ask for.*By providing you with this *serviec, I *hop I am *releiving one of the small details that seems so plentiful during tax time.

Please have *yuou accountant call me if he or she has any questions. *Inn addition, if I can offer any further assistance, *perwork, or real estate *advisee, please don't hesitate to call.

It is my goal to have you and your family as *client for life.

*sincerely,

Walter S. Sanford
PRESIDENT SGI

WSS/mer

FIGURE 1.18

Written Questions

Problem 1

What if the mortgage company was not meeting deadlines with regard to documents being issued or financing approved, and consequently a sale was in great jeopardy? What would you do to get the mortgage company to meet deadlines and save the sale?

Answer:

_____

_____

_____

_____

Problem 2

Walter has asked you to do two listing-packet (CMAs) and Monica has asked for two also. All four have equal value, and the listing presentations will be made that evening (Wednesday). During the day Walter calls in for two title packages and wants the info by the next afternoon.

The listing packets used by Walter and Monica are identical (and usually take 30 minutes each to prepare), but the supply of photocopied material usually used in them has been depleted. This information must be included in the listing packets for Wednesday evening.

It's Wednesday; you know that both Monica and Walter call all their clients on Thursday to relay the escrow update. You have 22 transactions in closing. During the day, both Walter and Monica are gone/out of phone contact. An agent on the selling side calls and informs you the appraisal on a certain property will be today at 2:00 P.M. Our seller is out of town and the door is locked. The home is 30 minutes from the office, and the key is in the office.

Please prioritize the day and develop three solutions to solve any problems—and don't forget to take lunch!

FIGURE 1.18 (Continued)

Answer:

_____

_____

_____

_____

Problem 3

Closing should have occurred on Monday, May 10th. It is now Friday, May 14th, and the sellers' moving van is ready to leave. The last detail is PMI (Private Mortgage Insurance) approval for the transaction to have closed so the sellers can be on their way to Washington.

The purchaser works for a PMI company. She has told the selling agent and the lender all along that she would have no problem getting PMI from her company. At 9:00 A.M. on Friday, May 14th, her own company turns her down. The selling agent calls at 9:05 A.M. and says to cancel the sale, because we can't get PMI. What would you do?

Answer:

_____

_____

_____

_____

FIGURE 1.19

The Perfect Assistant

How do you know if you've hired the perfect assistant? Sometimes the answer is not clear for a period of time, because only working with someone through a variety of situations tells you how he or she will really perform. There are several signals, however, that seem to be universal in what I call the "Profile of the Perfect Assistant."

- *Appearance*—A casual appearance denotes a casual regard for career. We require a business appearance at our office. We occasionally have casual days, but most of the time we require our assistants to be properly attired. Leggings, jeans, shorts, sleeveless tops, miniskirts and tennis shoes are not career apparel.

- *Learning*—An assistant who is constantly learning about real estate, listening to tapes, reading real estate magazines, reading books on real estate and always searching for new cutting-edge ideas to further the career of the agent he or she works for is a real asset.

- *Working Time*—Working 8 to 5 doesn't mean you arrive at 8 A.M.; it means you are ready to work at 8 A.M. Leaving at 5 doesn't mean your coat is on and your hand is on the door at 5 P.M. on the dot. Personal calls for five minutes may not seem like stealing to you, but you're cheating your boss. A ten-minute personal call each day multiplied by five days adds up to almost one hour a week you steal from your employer.

- *Discretion*—Everything that is said in the office about clients is confidential, of course. However, everything an assistant knows personally about the business and about the agent is also very confidential.

- *Team Player*—An assistant who is a team player and wants the success of the agent as much as the agent does is a truly valuable assistant. An assistant who is willing to do extra to ensure the success of the agent is irreplaceable.

- *Problem solving*—An assistant who solves problems and makes good decisions is extremely important to an agent.

FIGURE 1.19 (Continued)

- *Positive attitude*—It is great when an agent returns from a tough appointment feeling like fresh roadkill and the assistant is there to provide positive support. No matter what has happened to me during the day, Kim is always there smiling and happy, reminding me of my successes. It's not fun to work with someone glum who has a black cloud over his or her head.

- *Cut expenses*—The perfect assistant to me is always looking for ways to cut expenses, not create new ones just to make his or her job easier. The assistant is the perfect one to analyze all the expenses and determine if they can be eliminated or decreased.

- *Caring*—Agents I have surveyed across the United States all want the same thing. They want an assistant to care about the agent, about the quality of work, about the goals and, most important, about their job, always wanting to do their very best.

- *Initiative*—The ability to proceed on projects or tasks without supervision and instructions is a valuable quality. The assistant who can do this is truly irreplaceable!

2

Getting Your
Assistant Started

Once you've hired the perfect assistant, you quickly get into a jumble of issues most of us have not encountered before: motivating, training and setting policies. How can you make your assistant feel comfortable and also quickly become productive? Remember, you don't want to spend too much time working one-to-one; you'd rather give your new assistant a direction and some tools to work with, and then leave it to her or him to produce results.

Too often we focus on *how* people do their work rather than on the results. But you need to do the opposite to produce an environment in which your assistant can flourish. Once your goals are agreed upon, let people do things their own way for the most part.

On the assistant's first day, I strongly recommend clearing your calendar and devoting the day to providing explicit instructions and making necessary introductions. The first day on the job can determine your new hire's future success. I learned a few tips from some top producers that I would like to share with you. E.J. Simpson, RE/MAX, Walnut Creek, California, shared this great idea with me. The very first thing E.J. likes to share with his new assistant is why he hired her or him. Figure 2.1 is the letter he uses the first day to start everything off on a terrific note.

During orientation (Figure 2.2) you'll set the mood for the office and show them what kind of initiative you expect. One of the best ways of doing this is with our Shared Commitment form (Figure 2.3). This shows assistants what the office is providing and reveals what they in turn are willing to commit to you. Get it signed—and if your assistant starts feeling overworked at some later date, this is a good document to take out and review.

You'll also need to set clear policies on sick leave, a dress code, pay raises, vacations and holidays. You'll find suggestions on how to handle these important issues in Figures 2.6–2.8. You might want to have different policies; but make sure that whatever your policy is, it is clear from the outset. If you wait, your assistant might feel as though important matters were hidden from him or her.

Additionally, we suggest quickly impressing on your new assistant the chief reasons you have for dismissing people (Figure 2.9). Armed with that knowledge, your assistant can make a decision to be on the team and work for a common goal of making you more effective.

Policies and procedures are designed to provide goals and help focus your assistant's efforts. When combined with incentive pay, they help the assistant to grow. You don't want someone who just obeys the rules and shows up every day. You want an assistant who is actively doing everything he or she can to make the office more productive and profitable.

Our overriding goal, then, is to keep improving our productivity by working together.

WHY I HIRED YOU (FIGURE 2.1)

This form will validate the agent's selection process and also make the assistant feel very successful to be chosen over many qualified applicants. Hopefully, this subtle approach of congratulations gets everything off to the right start. Everyone wants to feel successful, and everyone likes to be complimented for a job well done.

ASSISTANT ORIENTATION CHECKLIST (FIGURE 2.2)

As I travel and speak to assistants throughout North America, I hear a common complaint about initial training. All too often, the first day on the job, the agent meets with the assistant for about 30 minutes and then is off and running. The dialogue usually consists of this: "Gosh, here are some of my listing files; why don't you look them over, and I'll answer your questions when I return." Well, the assistant is totally bewildered as to what to do next. This is hardly proper instruction or introduction to the office. Figure 2.2 is my orientation checklist and will provide the basics of what should be explained and discussed on day one. You will probably want to personalize it for yourself and your business.

I know of one assistant, newly hired, who was asked, "What are you looking for in the files, and who the heck are you anyway?" I call real estate offices frequently, and many times they do not know the assistant's name at the reception desk. Place some real importance on the first day. I suggest you spend the entire day setting the atmosphere for a successful team.

SHARED COMMITMENT (FIGURE 2.3)

This is a great form to utilize at the beginning of your relationship with your assistant, and for future reference too.

BUSINESS CARDS AND ANNOUNCEMENTS (FIGURE 2.4)

Because I feel it is very important that the assistant have her or his own business cards, I always order them on the first day. It validates the job and the importance of the assistant and also is a great prospecting tool. When assistants join our office, I ask them the very first day to write down 200 names and addresses of people in their sphere of influence. This can include people at their church or aerobics class, people they know at their child's day-care facility, neighbors, coworkers of their spouse, and so on. One assistant was able to come up with over 1,500 names. Now, that's a person who knows a lot of people!

The names are entered in the computer and coded to indicate that they are, for example, Kim's personal people farm. It is my firm belief that every assistant is a profit center/income generator for the agent. If an assistant brings at least two referrals per year to the agent, that assistant starts to pay for herself or himself. Once the names have been entered into the computer, I have the assistant mail-merge this announcement and get it ready to mail.

PRESS RELEASE (FIGURE 2.5)

The next thing on the agenda is the press release. We have our assistants familiarize themselves with the press release farm and then submit their first press release. A nice touch is to submit a picture of you and the assistant standing in front of a "Sold" sign announcing the new partnership that will enable you, the agent, to better service your clientele.

POLICY AND PROCEDURES

I could never remember year-to-year what holidays I had agreed to pay for, or exactly what policies I had established regarding vacations and bonuses.

Therefore, I encourage every agent to establish a policy and procedures manual. This will streamline the learning curve and also provide a great reference for all questions. If you establish a policy and procedures manual, you will never be hostage to any assistant because he or she is the only one who knows how the "expired program" works. Here are a few items you should include in your manual.

- Vacations
- Sick leave/pay
- Salary/bonuses
- Dress code
- Employee conduct
- Mission statement

PAY (FIGURE 2.6)

I firmly believe in hiring someone at a reasonable wage. Our range in California is between $8 and $15 per hour, though this figure will vary around the country. I then make it very clear that there are no raises. NO RAISES. This is a great way to eliminate the very uncomfortable situation of the assistant coming to you every three to six months for a raise of 25 cents or 50 cents. This can be very degrading and humiliating for both of you. I have found that incentives such as those in Figure 2.6 are a more challenging and professional way of increasing compensation by emphasizing merit and production.

I also really believe in the immediate-gratification system when an assistant does something extra-great. For instance, our assistant, Tori once had a choice to make. We had a very difficult seller, a really challenging person to work with. At the day of closing, the seller's proceeds check was to be available at 3:00 P.M. However, she had to work until 7:30 and couldn't pick it up. So Tori, instead of saying, "Well, I guess you'll get your check tomorrow," said, "No problem, we'll hire a messenger to deliver your check to your home at 8 o'clock tonight." That was definitely a "building a client for life" story, and Tori received a bonus for the extra effort. Furthermore, anyone who knows how difficult that person can be also knows that if she recommends Walter S. Sanford, he must really be a great agent.

DRESS CODE (FIGURE 2.7)

Now, there's a fun subject! I hope this section will be helpful to you so that you will always have established standards for employee appearance.

ABSENCES (FIGURE 2.8)

This form should help avoid any misunderstandings. It has been my observation that assistants can take advantage of personal days off. I had an assistant who seemed to call in sick once a month if not more. There are the exceptions, of course, and I take my hat off to those assistants. They are the best. The form is a log sheet that you can put in their personnel file for reference. Absences are very easy to document when you implement this form.

All I ask of my assistants is to inform me as far in advance as possible. If it is an emergency or illness, let me know first thing in the morning. I suggest that you definitely document absences.

REASONS FOR DISMISSAL (FIGURE 2.9)

I always provide this information to the new assistant the first day. I believe strongly in communicating the attitudes or behavior that will lead to dismissal.

FIGURE 2.1

Why I Hired You

I interviewed many applicants and I selected you for my team because:

I believe you to be someone who can set daily goals and achieve them.

I believe you to be someone who can set weekly, monthly, and yearly goals and achieve them.

I believe you to be on the same wavelength.

I believe you to be able to work smart.

I believe you to be someone with a great work ethic.

I believe you to be someone who won't question everything I do but will "take the ball and run."

I believe you to be someone who cares about quality of work.

I believe you to be someone who constantly thinks of ways to improve the office and our systems.

I believe you to be someone who will treat all clients with the utmost respect.

FIGURE 2.2

Assistant Orientation Checklist

Name: _____   Date: _____

_____ 1. Showed location of office equipment, coffee room, time clock, rest-room, bulletin boards.

_____ 2. Introduced to other coworkers in office.

_____ 3. Explained starting and quitting times, lunch hour, etc.

_____ 4. Indicated when and how paid.

_____ 5. Discussed overtime.

_____ 6. Discussed probationary period.

_____ 7. Informed where and when to call agent if absent.

_____ 8. Explained vacation and holiday pay.

_____ 9. Explained assistant's expected referral leads from assistant's people farm.

_____ 10. Gave a job description and duties for each day.

_____ 11. Read the office manual.

_____ 12. Listened to "Monica Reynolds at Your Assistance" tapes.

_____ 13. Listened to "The Real Estate Assistant as a Profit Center" tapes.

_____ 14. Explained no raises, just bonuses based on production.

_____ 15. Showed location of supplies.

_____ 16. Showed parking arrangements.

_____ 17. Showed how to use office equipment.

FIGURE 2.2 (Continued)

_____ 18. Gave computer instructions.

_____ 19. Demonstrated how to properly answer phone and handle clients.

_____ 20. Reviewed the assistant's manual.

Date Completed _____

Agent _____

Assistant _____

FIGURE 2.3

Shared Commitment

Assistant	Agent
	1. Paycheck
	2. Pleasant work environment
	3. Computer
	4. Desk
	5. Telephone
	6. Opportunities to make extra money
	7. Vacation time
	8. Personal time requests always considered
	9. A career . . . not a job
	10. Bonuses
	11. New challenges
	12. Flexibility
	13. Recognition
	14. Involvement in goal setting

Assistant: _____   Agent: _____

Date: _____   Date: _____

FIGURE 2.4

Assistant's People Farm Announcement

[*Date*]

[*TITLE*]   [*FIRST NAME*]   [*LAST NAME*]
[*MAILING ADDRESS*]
[*CITY*],   [*STATE*]   [*ZIP*]

Dear [*SALUTATION*]:

[*Your name*] is happy to announce that he/she has recently joined the real estate office of [*agent's name*]. [*your name*] will be assisting [*agent's name*], a top producer in the [*city*] area.

[*Your name*] is a member of [*clubs/organizations*]. His/Her wife/husband [*spouse's name*] is employed by [*employment*] and they have [*#*] children who attend [*schools*].

This new partnership will result in [*agent's name*] clients' properties being sold more efficiently and professionally and also at top market value.

Please call me at [*phone*] if [*your name*] or [*agent's name*] can be of any help to you with your real estate needs.

Sincerely,

[*Agent's Name*]

P.S. I have enclosed a postage-paid card if you would prefer to respond by mail.

FIGURE 2.5

Press Release for Your Assistant

Picture suggestion:

- Assistant only

- Assistant and agent with Sold sign

- Assistant with agent in front of office

[*Your name*] is happy to announce that
he/she has recently joined the real
estate office of [*agent's name*], a
top producer in the [*city*] area.
[*Your name*] is a member of [*(clubs*].
His/Her wife/husband [*spouse's name*]
is employed by [*employment*] and they
have (#) children, who attend [*schools*].
This new partnership will result in
[*agent's name*] clients' properties
being sold more effectively and professionally
and also at top market value.

FIGURE 2.6

Pay Schedule

1. Pay scales vary throughout the United States. An hourly wage for an assistant ranges from $8 to $15 in California.

2. A field coordinator or runner earns $6 per hour plus mileage.

3. Part-time employees earn $5–$6 per hour.

4. I love "kid power"! We pay $4–$5 per hour. My own kids worked for me from age five, when they stuffed envelopes in return for pizza and a movie. Kids aged 10–15 are excited to be "employed" and can deliver neighborhood flyers or prepare mailings.

5. I pay $25 for every lead generated that results in an appointment. For example, if the assistant is calling past clients and contacts a person who wants to speak to Walter about selling his home, and Walter goes out on the appointment, the assistant receives $25 whether or not this leads to the listing. This was a valid seller and Walter went on the appointment; therefore, the assistant is entitled to $25.

6. If the assistant brings a referral to the agent out of his or her sphere of influence, then the assistant is entitled to 20 to 25 percent of the commission minus expenses. Why not? This is definitely business that the agent would not have received any other way than through the assistant. This fee is called a bonus if the assistant is unlicensed.

7. We pay $100 at the close of each escrow if the assistant was responsible for obtaining the initial lead on the transaction.

8. We pay a $25–$50 bonus for every money-saving idea. This has saved us thousands over the years. We saved over $3,400 last year by reusing copier paper for first drafts.

9. Dinner or theater tickets for monthly goals met are a great bonus.

10. A monetary bonus or a paid vacation if an agent exceeds goals at the end of the year is also great.

FIGURE 2.6 (Continued)

11. We pay $100 at closing for a lead that was generated by an assistant's telemarketing.

12. We allow a paid day off for extra efforts that resulted in a great success.

13. Ask what the assistant would like that is extravagant. For example, Donna, a Marin County assistant, wants a diamond tennis bracelet. Thirty dollars of every closing goes into a savings account for her diamond bracelet. Now, that's a great way to keep assistants excited!

14. We also pay $100 for new lead-generating ideas.

FIGURE 2.7

Dress Standards

Minimum requirement for men:

- Dress shirt
- Slacks
- Shoes
- Ties (optional, but preferred)

Minimum requirement for women:

- Professional dress/slacks/skirts
- Coordinating blouses/sweaters/tops
- Hose/Nylons/Stockings
- Shoes

Minimum requirement for mailroom/field runner:

- Slacks/denim jeans
- Sport shirts/t-shirts/golf shirts
- Tennis shoes

Not acceptable:

- Biker shorts
- Leggings
- Torn blue jeans
- Short/crop tops
- Sheer tops
- Ungroomed appearance
- Fluorescent nail polish
- Advertisement t-shirts
- Unclean/wrinkled clothing

FIGURE 2.7 (Continued)

Responsibility:

Employees must dress in a manner that is consistent with their responsibilities, with particular attention to firm image and client interaction. Employees should address specific questions concerning dress code.

FIGURE 2.8

Vacation/Leave of Absence
Request and Approval

Employee Name: _____

Employee Hire Date: _____

Dates Requested for Vacation:

    First Choice: _____ to _____

    Second Choice: _____ to _____

Dates Requested for Leave of Absence:

_____ to _____

Reason for Leave Request: _____

_____

    Employee Signature: _____

    Date: _____

NOTE: If requesting a medical leave of absence, please attach copy of doctor's verification.

COMPANY USE ONLY!

Our records indicate that you have earned _____ days of vacation and are authorized to take _____ days per this request, which will result in a balance of _____ vacation days.

You are authorized _____ days of unpaid leave of absence.

We are pleased to have approved your vacation/leave of absence request.

    Authorized Approval: _____

    Date: _____

This form is placed in the employee file.

FIGURE 2.9

Thirty-one Reasons for Dismissal

1. Brings personal problems to the office.

2. Does not care about or take pride in his or her job.

3. Handles the agent's clients poorly.

4. Is always late and has a million excuses.

5. Is disorganized.

6. Misplaces or loses important paperwork or checks.

7. Displays negative attitude.

8. Complains about the workload.

9. Cannot handle pressure.

10. Is not capable of growing with job.

11. Has poor work habits.

12. Is dissatisfied with pay because of workload.

13. Does not pay for herself/himself.

14. Gossips in the office about agent's business/personal life.

15. Cannot perform job after adequate training.

16. Is not a team player.

17. Does not look for ways to bring business to agent.

18. Does not look for ways to cut expenses.

19. Is careless with supplies and expenses.

FIGURE 2.9 (Continued)

20. Is not willing to take on new responsibilities.

21. Constantly distorts truth.

22. Is a slow learner.

23. Never accepts responsibility for problems.

24. Never accepts responsibility for mistakes.

25. Displays improper etiquette.

26. Wears improper attire.

27. Loses temper.

28. Lacks loyalty.

29. Is dishonest.

30. Takes all the credit for agent's success.

31. Receives personal phone calls at work.

This is never an easy task, and we always try to improve and instruct an assistant rather than rehire. But never, never be held hostage. Remember, assistants are replaceable, but search for the one who is irreplaceable. Set your standards high!

Working Together, Achieving Goals

One of the major benefits of worksheets and checklists is to help us stay on the right track. In this chapter you'll find a variety of forms you can use right away to make sure your assistant is doing things that will help you make more money. You'll see how to communicate quickly and effectively and how to help your assistant formulate goals and keep priorities straight. Sample schedules are provided, along with forms to keep your office and your deals running smoothly. I've also included the monthly evaluation form we use for our assistants.

This chapter contains the most important information to address with your newly hired assistant. Most assistants who leave complain that the job was difficult and confusing. Agents do not always communicate clearly or include their assistants when they are setting goals. But when you go for a walk with someone, you go in the same direction, at the same pace and toward the same destination. This describes how you should work with your assistant.

Communicating job expectations, the job description, career goals and your view of the "big picture" will develop the team atmosphere necessary to keep your new assistant interested, enthusiastic and focused on a career with you. The forms are included in this chapter to assist you in overcoming the communication gap.

JOB DESCRIPTION (FIGURE 3.1)

This form makes certain your assistant knows what is expected of hir or her. By signing, they show that they agree to the activities listed on it. When you have a detailed job description such as this, there is no room for miscommunication or for your assistant to think "Gee, I didn't know the job was going to be like this!"

DAILY MEETING (FIGURE 3.2)

I suggest that this form be in a bright neon color to ensure that it won't get lost in a sea of white paper on our desks. Each evening before the assistant leaves, he or she can write down a few of the most important things that happened under "Yesterday I Did." Under "Today I Do" tomorrow's activities can be organized. This sheet also has a space to record problems or questions that can be addressed at quick, stand-up meetings in the morning.

GOAL-PLANNING WORKSHEET (FIGURE 3.3)

This worksheet is a form to use for long-term projects.

THINGS TO DO TODAY/GOAL (FIGURE 3.4)

This is an excellent way to break out steps so that your goal can be accomplished.

MONTHLY MEETING (FIGURE 3.5)

This particular form represents 14 areas in which we prospect and generate income. We set goals for each and monitor our progress each month. If we do not meet our goal, we look back on the activity of that month to determine why we were unsuccessful. When we meet or exceed our goal, we reflect back on the previous month's production to see if we should increase those efforts to achieve even greater success.

ACTIVITY CHART (FIGURE 3.6)

It is important to have a six-month plan listing important tasks that is visible at all times to both the agent and the assistant.

SAMPLE DAILY PLANNER (FIGURE 3.7)

Four pages of possible assistant daily planners are included here. It is important that an assistant have a written daily schedule. There will be many interruptions and fires to put out, of course, but it helps to have a daily schedule to refer to.

ASSISTANT SELF-EVALUATION (FIGURE 3.8)

This is a monthly critique to make sure assistants are on track in meeting goals, paying for themselves and providing money-making and money-saving ideas.

ASSISTANT PROGRESS REPORT (FIGURE 3.9)

Your assistant should fill out this report daily so you can monitor the progress of the assistant's prospecting efforts.

CLOSING/ESCROW REPORT (FIGURE 3.10)

Every Monday we check on each sale in process and update Walter with this information. This form also includes an update on the property management portion.

HEAD OF BUSINESS DEVELOPMENT (FIGURE 3.11)

This is another tracking form for monitoring the production of the assistant. We ask that the assistant fill out this form daily for Walter.

AGENT INFORMATION (FIGURE 3.12)

Important information about the agent is provided here so that tasks can be quickly delegated, such as ordering a rental car or flowers for someone.

THE TRAVEL CHECKLIST (FIGURE 3.13)

This checklist will allow your assistant to do many things for you prior to your leaving for a trip—and we all know what a busy time that is! It is also for your use, to make sure you have everything you need to make time away from the office productive.

BE PREPARED BOX (FIGURE 3.14)

The agent can delegate putting together a "minioffice" in a box to keep in his or her car. Included are such items as emergency listing files, stamps and personal brochures. It helps to always have everything you might need with you!

FIGURE 3.1

Job Description for Administrative Assistant

Goals—Why Tori Is Here:

1. To make sure clients are happy and satisfied with Walter's service.

2. To put Walter in front of as many buyers and sellers as possible, resulting in Tori paying for herself.

3. To look for ways to increase income and decrease expenses, resulting in Tori paying for herself.

4. To handle the administration and coordination of the office so Walter can focus on prospecting and selling real estate.

5. To make sure that the assistant and every other employee is a profit center by prospecting daily and asking for referrals.

6. To work hard, to understand Walter's goals and the way he thinks, and to try to think like he does.

Action Plan

1. AM/PM—All Expireds—Letters, calls and visits. Goal: To get Walter appointments!

2. Computer Backup—Once a week, Friday nights.

3. All Buyers—Call once a week; send properties and letters and do buyers' search.

4. Open Houses—Sundays, as often as possible.

5. Unit Mail-Out—Daily; 25 hand-typed letters to people who own five units or more. Then call the above 25 per day. Next day, new group of 25.

FIGURE 3.1 (Continued)

6. Fax/Modem—Daily; fax the new listings to real estate offices and update list with local prefixes.

7. Six-Month-Old FSBOs—Every Monday; research, library microfiche and call from old Sunday papers.

8. Local Professionals Farm—Every quarter; contact by letter and phone financial planners, accountants, lawyers, builders, architects.

9. Press Releases—Every two weeks; send to everyone on press release list; update and clean up list monthly.

10. Referral System—Monitor once a week; incoming and outgoing referrals, all correspondence and calls (agents and client referrals).

11. Research daily all free-and-clear newly listed apartment buildings and put on Walter's desk.

12. Board Breakfast Sheets—Thursday; "hot sheets" to printer ready for Tuesday's board breakfast.

13. I Saw You in the News, Congratulations—I send out 15–30 a week with a follow-up call.

14. Mark Burrell's Office—To learn Q&A, fax/modem.

15. Listing Leads A—Call weekly.

16. Current Listings—Call weekly.

17. Call "For Rents."

18. 25 Non-Owner-Occupied Letters—Daily; 25 follow-up calls daily.

I agree that this will make me productive and excited!

_____

Tori

FIGURE 3.2

Daily Meeting

Date: _____/_____

Yesterday I Did . . .

1. _____
2. _____
3. _____
4. _____
5. _____
6. _____
7. _____
8. _____

Today I Do . . .

1. _____
2. _____
3. _____
4. _____
5. _____
6. _____
7. _____
8. _____

Problems/Questions

1. _____
2. _____
3. _____
4. _____
5. _____
6. _____
7. _____
8. _____

FIGURE 3.3

Goal-Planning Worksheet

"Once you are moving in the direction of your goals . . . nothing can stop you."

Goal Statement:

_____

_____

_____

Start Date: _____ End Date: _____

- Ways I can measure progress on my goal:

  _____

  _____

  _____

- Obstacles to overcome:

  _____

  _____

  _____

- What sacrifices will be required:

  _____

  _____

  _____

- What benefits will result:

  _____

  _____

  _____

FIGURE 3.4

Things To Do Today

_____
(Priority)

_____　　　_____
(Date Established)　　　　　　　　(Deadline)

Goal

I want: _____

No later than: _____

Because (Benefit): _____

_____ *I promise myself* to work on this project in an organized manner until it is finished.

_____ *I will not* take on more than five projects at any one time.

Steps/To Do

_____　　_____

_____　　_____

_____　　_____

_____　　_____

Notes: _____

_____

_____

Remember to cross off those steps that you have completed.

FIGURE 3.5

Monthly Meeting

Date: _____

		Goal	Actual
1.	Listing presentations:	_____	_____
2.	Listings taken:	_____	_____
3.	In escrow:	_____	_____
4.	Closed #:	_____	_____
5.	FSBOs contacted:	_____	_____
6.	FSBOs listed:	_____	_____
7.	Expireds contacted:	_____	_____
8.	Expireds listed:	_____	_____
9.	People farm contacted:	_____	_____
10.	People farm listed:	_____	_____
11.	Past clients contacted:	_____	_____
12.	Past clients listed:	_____	_____
13.	Buyer calls:	_____	_____
14.	Buyers sold:	_____	_____

- Money-Saving Idea _____
- Money-Making Idea _____
- Time-Saving Idea _____
- Assistant Personal Referral Farm _____
- Referral _____

FIGURE 3.6

Activity Chart

#	ACTIVITY	JANUARY	FEBRUARY	MARCH	APRIL	MAY	JUNE
1	Brochure	X					
2	Market Trends						
3	Solicit Listings/Sales	X	X	X	X		X
4	Holiday						
5	Open House						
6	Past Clients	X	X	X	X X	X	X
7	Survey Questionnaire						
8	Just Listed/Sold/Reduc	X	X	X	X	X	
9	Promotional Events			X	X		
10	Advertising	X		X			
11	Newsletter	X	X	X	X	X	X
12	Press Release						
13	Writing						
14	Printing						
15	Followup	X		X	X	X	
16	Budgeting						
17	Vacations/Days Off						
18	Personal/Family						
19	Seminar	Mom's BD		X convention		Anniversary	
20	Special Days	X				X	

FIGURE 3.6 (Continued)

ACTIVITY	JANUARY	FEBRUARY	MARCH	APRIL	MAY	JUNE	
1							1
2							2
3							3
4							4
5							5
6							6
7							7
8							8
9							9
10							10
11							11
12							12
13							13
14							14
15							15
16							16
17							17
18							18
19							19
20							20

FIGURE 3.7

Sample Daily Planner
from July 6

Time	MONDAY, JULY 6 188/178	TUESDAY, JULY 7 189/177	WEDNESDAY, JULY 8 190/176
7			
7:15			
7:30			
7:45			
8	Check Desk For Priorities /	Check Desk for Priorities	← Same
8:15	Ans Machine	Ans Machine	
8:30	Meet w / Agent	Meet w / Agent	← Same
8:45			
9			
9:15		Handle Priorities	
9:30	Handle Priorities		Handle Priorities
9:45			
10			
10:15	Process New Listings		Call Escrows
10:30			
10:45			
11	Call Buyers for		Deliver
11:15	Updates	Realtor Open	Press Release
11:30	Open House Attendees	House	Banking
11:45			Lock Boxes
12			
12:15	Lunch		Lunch
12:30		Lunch	
12:45			
1	Errands, Lock Boxes,	Call All	Call Ad For
1:15	Keys	Listings for	Open House
1:30	Drive By New Listings —	Agent	Do Flyers / Org.
1:45	Leave Brochures		Signs
2		Meet w / Affiliates	Send Realtor
2:15	Correspondence	to go over	Evaluation Forms
2:30		teamwork!	Deliver Flyers,
2:45	Pay Bills		go to Printer
3	Monitor	Do CMA's	Send Buyers
3:15	Escrow Files	For Weds.	Current Info
3:30		Appt	
3:45			
4	Call Expireds	Call Expireds /	Call Expireds —
4:15		FSBO's	
4:30	Past Clients		6 Month Old
4:45		Rtn Calls	Expireds
5	Rtn End of Day		Planning for
5:15	Calls /		Thurs. / Rtn
5:30	Organize Desk for Tomorrow	Org Desk / Plan for Wed	Calls
5:45			
6			
6:15			
6:30			
6:45			
7			
7:15			
7:30			
7:45			
8			
8:15			
8:30			
8:45			

FIGURE 3.7 (Continued)

to July 12

THURSDAY, JULY 9 191/175	FRIDAY, JULY 10 192/174	SATURDAY, JULY 11 193/173
7	7	7
7:15	7:15	7:15
7:30	7:30	7:30
7:45	7:45	7:45
8 Check Desk for	8	8
8:15 Priorities / Ans Mach	8:15 Same	8:15 Same
8:30	8:30 →	8:30 Just Kidding!
8:45 Meet w Agent	8:45	8:45
9	9 Handle	9
9:15	9:15 Top	9:15
9:30 TOP Priorities	9:30 Priorities	9:30
9:45	9:45	9:45
10	10 Attend Closing	10
10:15	10:15	10:15 DAY
10:30 Send Out	10:30	10:30
10:45 Just Listed/	10:45	10:45
11 Just Sold	11 Write Press Releases	11
11:15 Cards	11:15	11:15
11:30	11:30	11:30
11:45	11:45	11:45 OFF
12	12	12
12:15	12:15 Wash / gas Agent's	12:15
12:30 Lunch	12:30 Car / Lunch	12:30
12:45	12:45	12:45
1 Process	1 Update Transaction	1
1:15 New Listings	1:15 Report / Sales /	1:15
1:30	1:30 Listings	1:30
1:45 Rtn Calls	1:45	1:45
2	2	2
2:15 Order Stationery	2:15 Process New Listings	2:15
2:30 Type All	2:30	2:30
2:45 Correspondence	2:45 Due Emergency CMA	2:45
3	3 Write Thank-you's	3
3:15 Prepare Closing	3:15	3:15
3:30 for Friday	3:30 Call Expireds /	3:30
3:45	3:45	3:45
4 Call Expireds /	4 Past Clients /	4
4:15 Buyers	4:15	4:15
4:30	4:30 Listing Leads A	4:30
4:45	4:45	4:45
5 Planning /	5 Planning / Organizing	5
5:15 Organizing For	5:15 For Friday	5:15
5:30 Friday!	5:30 Rtn Calls	5:30
5:45	5:45	SUNDAY, JULY 12 194/172
6	6	
6:15	6:15	
6:30	6:30	
6:45	6:45	
7	7	2:00 OPEN HOUSE
7:15	7:15	For Realtor
7:30	7:30	At 7750 S. 7th St.
7:45	7:45	4:00
8	8	
8:15	8:15	
8:30	8:30	
8:45	8:45	

FIGURE 3.8

Assistant Self-Evaluation

1. How did you pay for yourself?

2. How did you develop goals?

3. How did you become the CEO of your job?

4. How did you make Walter look good?

5. Who relied on you?

6. What additional jobs did you accept that made others' jobs easier?

7. What extra items did you do this month?

8. Was your listing package successful?

9. What did you do to guarantee a customer for life?

10. If you were the president of this group, what would you do differently?

11. What is one money-making idea for this company for cutting expenses?

12. What is one money-making idea for this company for increasing income?

FIGURE 3.9

Assistant Progress and Goal Daily Report

Day: _____   Date: _____

1. Clients-for-life successes:

    •

    •

    •

2. Personal referrals: _____

3. Daily escrow update: Needs, problems, discussions, close date (over)

4. Tenant 3-day/promise (over)

5. Tenant letters out: • New: # _____

                                    • Referral request: # _____

6. CMAs completely done: # _____

7. Pre-com packages out: # _____

8. New listings completely processed: # _____

9. Sales completely closed: # _____

10. Surveys sent: • Coop agents: # _____

                             • Clients: # _____

11. Anniversary letters out: # _____

12. Special letters out: # _____

13. Special programs progress: _____

14. Buyer showings: # _____

15. Tenant showings: # _____

16. Open house progress: _____

17. Class B mailings ordered: # _____

FIGURE 3.9 (Continued)

18. Buyer Report (Thursday): _____

19. Mail—LPs sent: # _____

20. New escrows opened: # _____

21. Ads placed: # _____

22. Complaints taken: # _____

23. Brochures completed: # _____

24. Listing leads taken: # _____

25. Rents taken:

Name	Address	Amount
•		
•		
•		
•		
•		
•		

26. Tenant Outgoing 3-Day Notice Report

_____ Date/$ _____ Total _____

Tenant	Address	Promise	Amt Owed*
•			
•			
•			
•			
•			

* Total amount owed includes all rent, unpaid deposits, late charges, NSF fees and attorney.

27. WSS: _____ BM: _____

FIGURE 3.10

Closing/Escrow Report

	Address	Client	Problems/Solutions	Estimated Closing Date
1.				
2.				
3.				
4.				
5.				
6.				
7.				
8.				
9.				
10.				
11.				
12.				
13.				
14.				
15.				
16.				
17.				
18.				
19.				
20.				

FIGURE 3.11

Head of Business Development
Control Record and Progress Report

Day: _____

Date: _____

1. **Expireds:** • regular letters out # _____
   - • phone calls # _____   • special letters out # _____
   - • personal visits # _____   • expired watch # _____

2. **Computer backup:** • completed # _____
   - • problem: _____

3. **Unit mailout:** • letters out # _____
   - • phone calls made # _____ from batch date: _____

4. **Fax modem:** • new listings # _____   • changes # _____

5. **One-fifth of this week's** six-month-old FSBO calls: # _____

6. Progress on this week's OH: _____

7. Progress on this mo. pro. farm: _____

8. Progress on #1/#2 (circle one) Press release this mo.: _____

   _____

9. Referral update calls (Outgoing—mark on files) # _____

10. Offers faxed #: _____

11. Progress on Board Breakfast sheets: _____

12. "Saw you in the news" letters out #: _____

13. LLA calls #: _____ (Record on file)

14. One-fifth of this week's for-rents: • letters # _____
    - • calls # _____

15. 25 Non-Own-Occ.: • letters out# _____   • phone calls made
    # _____ from batch date _____

FIGURE 3.11 (Continued)

16. FSBO:
    - week 1–2 letters # _____ + calls # _____
    - week 3–4 letters # _____ + calls # _____
    - week 5–6 letters # _____ + calls # _____
    - week 7–8 letters # _____ + calls # _____
    - week 9–10 letters # _____ + calls # _____

17. Tickler file calls #: _____

18. Class B Mailouts #: _____ (Call mail house)

19. Past clients calls connected:
    - # _____
    - letters out _____

20. Have/want calls made #: _____

21. Personal referrals developed:
    - appt. # _____
    - up cards # _____

22. Six-month-old expireds called #: _____

23. One major event progress: _____

24. Special project progress: _____

	Leads (up cards)#	Appointments
Today		
Week		
Month		
Year		

#1 Int. _____ #2 Int. _____ #3 Int. _____ #4 Int. _____

FIGURE 3.12

Agent Information

Full Name: _____

Birthdate: _____ Social Sec. # _____

Spouse Full Name: _____ Anniver: _____

Children: _____

Home Address: _____

_____

Phone—

Home Phone: _____ Fax: _____

Spouse Work #: _____ Car Phone: _____

Emergency Phone: _____

Contact Name: _____ Relation: _____

Neighbor Name/Address/Phone: _____

_____

Neighbor Name/Address/Phone: _____

_____

Financial—

MasterCard: _____ Exp. _____

VISA: _____ Exp. _____

American Express: _____ Exp. _____

_____ : # _____

_____ : # _____

Savings Bank: _____ Contact: _____

Address: _____

Phone: _____ Acct #: _____

FIGURE 3.12 (Continued)

Checking Bank: _____   Contact: _____

Address: _____

Phone: _____   Acct #: _____

Automated Teller Card:# _____

Code:# _____

Insurance—

Company: _____

Contact Name: _____   Phone: _____

Policy Number: _____

Car License Number: _____

Miscellaneous Information—

Tailor: _____   Phone: _____

Accountant: _____   Phone: _____

Hairstylist: _____   Phone: _____

Florist: _____   Phone: _____

Athletic Club: _____   Phone: _____

Restaurants: • _____   Phone: _____

• _____   Phone: _____

• _____   Phone: _____

Rental Car Style: 1st _____   2nd _____

Hotel: Smoking room _____   Nonsmoking _____   Level _____

Airline: Smoking _____   Nonsmoking _____   Coach/1ST/Window

Carwash: _____

Shirt Size: _____   Pant Size: _____

Shoe Size: _____   Dress: _____

FIGURE 3.13

The Travel Checklist

Things To Do Before You Leave

____ Call airlines 21 days prior to departure for best rates.

____ Call hotel to make reservations.

____ Write down all confirmation numbers.

____ Get travelers checks.

____ Make a list of emergency numbers for your family.

____ Pay all your bills.

____ Arrange to have your car serviced.

____ Leave some petty cash and three signed checks.

____ Give extra prospecting duties to your assistant with accountability.

____ Arrange for specific call-in times with your assistant or the person covering for you.

____ Change your voice mail message if necessary.

____ Leave the phone and fax number of your hotel.

____ Arrange for car rental.

Things You Can't Go Without

____ Your business cards

____ Your confirmation numbers for the hotel

____ Airline tickets

____ Car rental information

____ Your day-timer

____ Marketing materials

____ Your checkbook

FIGURE 3.13 (Continued)

_____ Your credit cards

_____ Travelers checks

_____ Referral material

_____ Writing pens and highlighters

_____ Microcassette recorder

_____ Camera and film

_____ Four comfortable layered outfits

_____ Golf clubs, tennis racket, etc.

_____ Swimsuit

_____ Toiletry kit

_____ Glasses (prescription & sun)

_____ Any medications

_____ A "need" to network

_____ Your assistant

Things To Do When You Get There

_____ Network.

_____ Pay attention.

_____ Call at your appointed times.

_____ Review your notes in the evening, picking out the two best items to implement.

_____ Make five new friends in different areas of the country.

_____ Keep an open mind.

_____ Call your family and tell them you're working hard.

_____ Complete day-timer for new projects you're excited about.

_____ Exercise and eat well.

_____ Have fun!!!

FIGURE 3.14

Be Prepared Box

____	1.	Deposit receipt	____	24. Heet
____	2.	Chalk	____	25. Evian
____	3.	Rope	____	26. Small tool kit
____	4.	Thank-you notes	____	27. 2 Lockboxes
____	5.	Marbles so floors are even	____	28. "Sold" riders
____	6.	Flashlight	____	29. Open-House riders
____	7.	Tape measure at least 50 feet or rolling	____	30. Brochure box
____	8.	Mallet or hammer	____	31. Brochure caddy
____	9.	Vanilla extract	____	32. Pop-up wipes
____	10.	Toilet paper	____	33. $5 in quarters
____	11.	Stamps	____	34. $5 in $1 bills
____	12.	Legal pad	____	35. Fix-a-Flat
____	13.	Buyer net sheet	____	36. Air freshener
____	14.	Seller net sheet	____	37. Facial tissues
____	15.	Disclosure forms	____	38. Paper towels
____	16.	Listing agreements	____	39. Scotch tape
____	17.	Personal brochures	____	40. Small stapler
____	18.	Business cards	____	41. Paperclips
____	19.	Business-reply cards	____	42. Agent roster
____	20.	Pens, pencils, calculator	____	43. Past MLS Book
____	21.	Coloring book, crayons	____	44. Five property brochures for each listing
____	22.	Marking pens	____	45. Can of Mace
____	23.	WD 40	____	46. Matches

FIGURE 3.14 (Continued)

_____ 47. Microcassette recorder tape

_____ 48. Breath spray, chewing gum

_____ 49. Camera

_____ 50. Film for camera

_____ 51. Batteries for camera

_____ 52. Five firecrackers for FSBO

_____ 53. Videotapes, personal brochures

_____ 54. FSBO kits

_____ 55. Scissors

_____ 56. Swiss Army knife

_____ 57. Dog biscuits

_____ 58. Dog-Away spray

_____ 59. Whistle

_____ 60. Emergency listing file

4

Effective Use
of the Telephone

The telephone is the most important piece of equipment in the office of a real estate agent. The impression made in the first ten seconds of a call is critical. On the following pages, I share with you our answering techniques, words to use and avoid, and telephone tips.

It's sometimes difficult to remember that the telephone is the REALTOR'S® best friend for business. It enables you to stay in touch with your clients and prospects. This is how you deliver your messages, products and services. It's how you prospect for and conduct everyday business. It's also how you increase your business.

Yet, most of us look at the phone as the enemy when it rings. When we make calls, the continual ringing, busy signals and being put on hold for the fourth time make us dislike the phone. If that isn't enough, there are the people who don't call you back, people who never stop calling, irate callers, messages that pile up and phone tag. These types of calls compounded with an extremely busy day make you want to go over to the desk and pull the phone out of the wall. I feel like this at least three times a day!

The following hints and tips are designed to help you deal with the many telephone problems. These ideas will help you be more productive, do a better job and even suffer a little less when all those lights start blinking at once!

TELEPHONE-ANSWERING TECHNIQUES (FIGURE 4.1)

When you have 168 listings like Walter, you need to know who the caller is and why they are calling. Walter doesn't remember one seller from another! Could that be true of you? Wouldn't it be great to always know who is calling and why before you pick up the phone? This could save you an embarrassing moment.

MESSAGES (FIGURE 4.2)

Walter never returns a telephone call himself. They are placed for him. All messages are returned. If the caller is not in, a message is left.

PHONE PHRASES TO AVOID AND HELPFUL ALTERNATIVES (FIGURE 4.3)

You depend on the phone to bring in calls from buyers and sellers. You use the phone to speak to lenders, appraisers, inspectors and escrow agents. The phone line is literally your lifeline. Obviously, phone skills are vital to your success. Here are some phrases you might not want to say.

LEVEL-ELEVATING WORDS (FIGURE 4.4)

Level-elevating words raise the other person to a level above the ordinary—a plus for anyone who has contact with an agent's clients. Here are ten examples.

TELEPHONE POLICY CHECKLIST (FIGURE 4.5)

Here are some great points to remember when answering the phone!

TAG, YOU'RE IT (FIGURE 4.6)

Telephone tag is a game played every day in offices everywhere. Some people are real pros at it. Here's how to end the, "I'm returning her call returning my call returning her call from yesterday" routine.

"HOLD, PLEASE" (FIGURE 4.7)

The hold button is a fascinating feature. When we're placed on hold, we hate it. But when we can put people on hold, we love it.

YOUR THREE MINUTES ARE UP (FIGURE 4.8)

Here are some helpful hints when *you* are left on hold or to avoid wasting time.

FIGURE 4.1

Telephone-Answering Techniques

Initial call:

"Good morning/afternoon/evening. Walter Sanford's office, Margaret speaking. May I help you?"

All calls should be directed to the assistant. This is vital. It eliminates unnecessary calls to the agent.

"Walter is not available at this time. Can his assistant Monica help you?"

If the caller has been on hold:

"Good morning/afternoon/evening. Thank you for waiting, may I help you?"

Caller wishes to speak with Walter. This is *always* the next question whether Walter is available or not: "Would it be helpful to Walter to know what this call is regarding?"

If Walter is not available:

"Thank you for calling. I will make sure Walter receives your message."

The assistant can return these calls and free up a tremendous amount of time for the agent. The agent speaks to a "connected" call or the assistant leaves a message.

"Good morning/afternoon/evening, Mr. Smith. I have Walter Sanford on the line and he wishes to speak with you. Could you hold a moment, please?"

Answer the Phone Clearly!

If you were to call businesses at random to see how their phones were answered, in far too many cases the person answering would butcher the company name, slide over it, mumble it or speak so fast that the name is lost. Don't assume people know where they're calling. They may be returning a call and have only your phone number. Besides, answering clearly is just good manners.

FIGURE 4.2

Messages

"Please tell Mr. Smith that Walter Sanford returned his call and would like him to call Walter at his earliest convenience."

All calls are returned within three hours.

Keeping unnecessary phone calls away from the agent

Problem-solving examples:

#1—Agent Call

Agent:	"Is Walter in?"
Assistant:	"Yes, but he is in a conference with a client. May I help you? I'm his assistant, Monica."
Agent:	"Does 268 Belmont have a two-car attached or detached garage?"
Assistant:	"I can help with that information. That home has a two-car detached. Are there any other questions I can help you with today?"
Solution:	Agent call successfully solved by assistant.

#2—Call from Lender with Potential Disaster!

Ms. Lender:	"I need to speak with Walter; 3478 Main Street is falling apart."
Assistant:	"Ms. Lender, please tell me the particulars so I can give Walter a detailed message."
Ms. Lender:	"Three late payments on two different credit cards."
Assistant:	"What are three possible solutions?"
Ms. Lender:	(Tells assistant what could possibly be done to cure this problem.)
Assistant:	• Notifies buyers of problem and possible solutions and has them call lender to begin process. • Tells Walter the problem and solutions. • Follows up with buyer and lender.
Solution:	Assistant solves all!

FIGURE 4.2 (Continued)

#3—*Distressed Seller*

Assistant: "Good morning, Walter Sanford's office. How may I help you?"

Seller: "This is John Donut. I need to speak with Walter immediately; it's very, very important!"

Assistant: "I'm sorry, Walter is on a long distance phone call. May I help you? I'm his assistant, Monica."

Seller: "No, I must speak with him!"

Assistant: "Mr. Donut, please give me a message as to what this is regarding, and I will make sure Walter sees the message as soon as he is off the phone."

Seller: "Well, my sign blew down. I need someone to put it back up immediately."

Assistant: "Mr. Donut, I will have that problem corrected today. I will call the sign company now and have that problem solved by 5 P.M. Is there anything else I can do for you?"

Seller: "My brochure box is out of flyers."

Assistant: "Great! I will bring more flyers by today on my way home."

Seller: "Good! Well, I guess I don't need to speak to Walter after all."

Assistant: "Thank you for calling. I will personally attend to these matters. Have a nice day!"

Solution: "Mr. Donut happy! Assistant solves problem, Walter not bothered with this detail!"

#4—*Personal Travel Plans*

Agent: Plans to travel to real estate seminar.

Assistant: Gets dates, schedules plane and rental car if necessary, reserves room, sends in registration and check, and gives itinerary to agent.

Solution: No agent involvement.

#5—*Termite Disaster*

Agent: Termite company called; please call back ASAP!

Assistant: Call for agent, get all facts regarding problem and solution, tell agent if necessary.

FIGURE 4.2 (Continued)

Assistant: Call back termite company with solution and notify all parties involved.

Solution: No agent involvement.

#6—Distressed Seller

Seller: "May I speak with Walter?"

Assistant: "I'm sorry, Walter is in conference now. May I help you? I'm his assistant, Monica."

Seller: "Sure! When is my property at 340 Grand going to be advertised in the *Press Telegram*?"

Assistant: "I can help you with that! We have scheduled an ad for next week. We will be sending you a copy. Is there anything else I can help you with today?"

Seller: "No, that's it."

Assistant: "Thank you for calling. Please call again if I can answer any of your questions."

Solution: No agent involvement.

#7—Key Disaster

Call to agent: Key missing from lockbox and showing agent wants to show the property tomorrow.

Assistant: Takes spare copy and makes another key, puts in lockbox prior to promised time for the showing.

Solution: Assistant solves problem!

#8—Appraisal Question for Agent

Agent calls: Appraiser wants comparables for newly sold listing.

Assistant: Pulls newly sold properties from computer and faxes to appraiser.

Agent: Not involved!

FIGURE 4.3

Phone Phrases To Avoid
and Helpful Alternatives

"I don't know."   There is no need to ever utter these three words. If you don't know, FIND OUT. That's your job. There isn't a thing you can't find out, outside of sensitive and financial information.

Instead: *"Gee, that's a good question.* Let me check and find out." Then go find out.

"We can't do that."   This one is guaranteed to get your customer's blood boiling.

Instead: *"Boy, that's a tough one. Let's see what we can do."* Then find an alternative solution. Never, never repeat the negative—there's no need to remind the caller of what you *CAN'T* do. Tell the caller what you *CAN* do; you'll find an acceptable alternative solution 98 percent of the time. When it looks as if you're absolutely unable to help, come back with, "I sure tried for you, but it looks like you may have us on that one." Then ask if the caller has any suggestions. Often their request is easy to handle.

"You'll have to. . . ."   Wrong. The only thing the caller has to do is die and pay taxes. Tell callers what they have to do and rest assured they won't.

Instead: Soften the request. Use phrases such as *"you'll need to"* or *"here's how we can help with that"* or *"the next time that happens, here's what you could do."* Remember, we take orders from our clients; we don't give them.

"Hang on a second, I'll be right back."   If you've ever said that to a caller, you lied. Not a big lie, but an unnecessary lie. Anyway, it's very rude.

Instead: Watch what happens when you tell the truth. *"It may take two or three minutes to get that information. Can you hold while I check?"* This one is a real crowd-pleaser and lessens the pain of being put on hold. Once callers know why they are holding, they are much more willing to accommodate you.

"No" at the beginning of a sentence   The word "no" conveys total re-jection, and most sentences can be grammatically correct without it. This isn't

FIGURE 4.3 (Continued)

as easy as it sounds. For example, when asked "Have you ever been to North Dakota?" one would probably answer, "No, I haven't." But it would be just as correct to say, "I haven't been there yet." That's much more pleasing to the ear.

Instead: If you think before you speak, you can turn every answer into a positive response. Another example: *"We aren't able to put the sign up tomorrow, but we can do that by Tuesday."*

You'll be amazed at the difference you can make by simply eliminating these five phrases. Once you've perfected them at the office, try them on your spouse and children—they work wonders at home, too!

FIGURE 4.4

Level-Elevating Words

"May I?"—Asking permission implies authority.

"As you of course know"—Implies vast knowledge and validates their intelligence.

"I'd like your advice"—Suggests superior wisdom.

"I'd sure appreciate it if . . ."—The implication here is that he or she has the power to refuse or grant.

"You are so right"—A pat on the back.

"Can you spare time from your busy life?"—Implies he or she is busy and, therefore, an important person.

"Because of your specialized knowledge"—Implies skill and professionalism.

"A person of your standing"—No one knows just what standing means, but everyone believes (or hopes) he or she has it.

"I'd like your considered opinion"—People on pedestals are supposed to have opinions, so if an opinion is asked, the person must be up there somewhere.

"Please"—A great lubricator in human relations.

Level-elevating words: Use them—and watch your popularity grow!

FIGURE 4.5

Telephone Policy Checklist

_____ 1. When the phone rings, *always* put a smile on your face! People know by the tone of your voice whether you are enjoying what you are doing or not. We want to keep the idea that this (like Disneyland!) is a happy place to work.

_____ 2. Always answer enthusiastically: "It's a great day at the Sanford Group! How may I help you?"

_____ 3. When answering phone calls, always ask the caller: "Would it be helpful if _____ knew what this call was regarding?"

_____ 4. When making phone calls for Walter, you say: "Good (morning, afternoon, evening) Mr/Mrs. _____. Walter Sanford asked me to get you on the line to discuss [property address] or _____ look at lead classification. (Example FSBO, Expired, Past Expired) Would you please hold for one moment while I get him on the line?"

_____ 5. Give call to party the caller is asking for. Always ask permission to put caller on hold, and wait for an answer.

_____ 6. If that party is not in or is on another line, ask if someone else can help. For example: "Walter is on another line. Can I help you at this time?"

_____ 7. If no one is available and you have to take a message, take the following required information from the caller:
   • *Name*—Ask the caller politely how to spell his or her name.
   • *Phone number* where caller can be reached—be sure to get both a work and home number, and repeat each number to be certain it's correct.
   • *Message*—Please find out why they are calling and be specific! You can say something like, "Walter usually calls in for his messages, and he may be able to answer the question and have me call you back."

Note: Do not push callers too hard, but try to get the most information out of them.

_____ 8. During the conversation with the caller, always be polite by adding "*thank you*" and "*please.*" Never be demanding or rude.

_____ 9. No matter how badly you are treated by someone on the phone, they are always potential clients and are *always* right.

FIGURE 4.6

Tag, You're It

- Return phone calls about ten minutes before noon and ten minutes before 5 PM. Most people are in their offices at those times.

- When people you call aren't in, ask what is the best time to reach them on most days.

- Don't just leave a message when someone isn't available. See if another decision maker is available.

- If you do leave a message, make it clear when you will be available. If you're going to be away from your phone for the next few hours, make sure that's included with the message.

- If you just need some information, leave a message that suggests what to do if you're not in when they call back.

FIGURE 4.7

"Hold, Please"

Hold is probably the most powerful weapon in the telephone arsenal, so use it with extreme care. What happens when a caller is placed on hold? Most people will hang up after about 40 seconds if they're paying for the call. People calling an 800 number will hold for about three minutes.

- Never put a person on hold until you've asked permission to do so. Wait for the answer.

- People will hold longer if they know the name of the person they're holding for, so tell them who will be answering. You might say, "If you'll please hold, I'll let Mary Smith know you're returning her call."

- Beware of the irate caller. That person will stay on hold forever—and get angrier with each second.

FIGURE 4.8

Your Three Minutes Are Up

Phones can be the biggest time-waster in the office.

Here are some time-savers.

• When you're stuck on the phone with a well-meaning prospect, after the business conversation has come to an end, find a polite way to end the call. For example: "I just noticed it's 2:15 and I have a report due by 2:30," or "Just one more question before we hang up."

• When you need to return a phone call from someone who tends to talk too much, begin the conversation with something like, "Hi, I have three questions for you."

• If someone asks to put you on hold, say "Fine, as long as you take down my number. I'm expecting a call and I may have to hang up." You'll be less likely to get lost on hold that way.

• Consider using a headset or shoulder rest if you spend a great deal of time on the phone. You'll find these devices make long periods on the phone less stressful, as your hands will be free to take notes or complete other tasks.

5

Telemarketing

Will Rogers said, "There ain't no second chance at first impressions." It is impossible to speak with someone over the phone and not picture what they look like. If we get a good mental image of someone, then we're more inclined to want to meet them face to face. All of us have been surprised at meeting people face to face whom we mentally pictured much differently from their phone voice image. Our voices paint a picture of what we look like. How do you want people to perceive you?

Walter Cronkite was once voted the most trustworthy person in America. Remember his voice? His tonality just exuded confidence and veracity. We never knew what he personally thought about a topic because he presented the news in such an unbiased manner. We believed what he said. Have you ever realized how many different tones of voice we use throughout the day? We use different tones with different people. Think of the different way you talk to babies, teen-agers, parents, spouses, bosses and clients. Think of the way you sound when you're excited, scared, happy, angry and satisfied.

WHY SCRIPTS?

Have you ever had a conversation with someone and then afterward, in your car on the way home, thought of some other important points you should have covered? Were you upset that you didn't think of them at the time of your conversation? Did those forgotten ideas possibly cost you a sale or appointment? How can you ensure that it doesn't happen again?

Since people began speaking in public, professionals have understood the importance of writing their thoughts down in scripts and practicing before delivery. Politicians, doctors, teachers and professional salespeople have all developed scripts, practiced their delivery and then presented their thoughts to their audience.

The majority of salespeople have never learned how effective it is to use a preplanned script when telemarketing. They assume that telemarketing is just a matter of asking the right questions under pressure. What usually happens is that they're so busy trying to think of their next question that they're not listening to the response to the last question. A script will relieve telemarketers of the pressure of thinking what to say next and allow them to hear the responses and tune into the prospect.

Anticipating what to say and how to say it to sellers and buyers can definitely make you more successful. Prepare for the call. Know what outcome you want. Imagine the conversation you'd like to have. Imagine the conversation that will accomplish your goals. Write them down. Consider the responses you might hear from the other person. Determine your best response, write it down and practice it. As you speak, let your fingers follow your script. *Leave your mind relaxed for listening.*

Having good phone scripts allows an assistant to handle many incoming phone calls without disturbing the agent. In this chapter you'll find scripts for everything from the routine to disasters.

It's important that you and your assistant understand Federal Communications Commission regulations regarding telemarketing. The following are important features.

- If someone you have "cold called" asks one of your telemarketers not to call him or her in the future, then you must take that household off all lists that any of your callers are using.
- You can't call homes before 8 AM or after 9 PM.
- A written statement on your firm's calling policy must be developed and adhered to.
- You cannot send unsolicited sales matter over fax machines, computers or phones to other electronic equipment.
- Prerecorded messages are not to be used on any residence unless a business relationship is established.

Some states have additional laws covering telemarketing that must be followed.

As you will read in later chapters, your assistant will be a major prospecting center for you. Forms are here to help assistants develop phone scripts for themselves. Sample telemarketing scripts also are included for FSBOs and an assistant's people farm.

WORDS TO AVOID/WORDS TO USE (FIGURE 5.1)

Have you ever had a conversation with a doctor and not understood a word he or she said? Or talked with your auto mechanic, electrician or insurance salesperson and had to ask them to explain what they mean? Use of presumptive terminology is another classic mistake made by inexperienced agents. In an effort to impress prospects with their vast knowledge of real estate, agents all too often lose their prospects with confusing verbiage. This occurrence is compounded by the fact that they cannot see their prospects and therefore cannot tell from their body language that they're lost.

Remember when you first started in real estate? Did you understand all of the terminology? Would they need you if they really understood it all? Try to eliminate as many technical terms as possible and make sure that you're understood on your key points.

Will Rogers also said, "I never get in a car and drive away until I'm sure everyone is in." Make sure your prospects are with you.

In addition to technically confusing terms, words with a negative connotation should be avoided.

NO, NO MONOTONE (FIGURE 5.2)

Nobody wants to listen to someone with a monotone voice. An enthusiastic, lively voice is the first step toward being successful. Your voice is the only contact you'll make with prospects. If you've got a good-sounding voice with a little sparkle, you'll make a good first impression. When your voice sounds great, you'll feel great about what you are doing. Keep these points in mind to develop a good voice personality.

CONTROL YOUR ENVIRONMENT (FIGURE 5.3)

Being certain that your working environment is comfortable makes a big difference in your voice when you are telemarketing! Here are some ideas that might help.

FIVE QUALITIES OF A GOOD TELEPHONE VOICE (FIGURE 5.4)

Why is it so pleasant to talk with some people and not with others? These tips might make *you* easier to listen to, and make you more successful.

WHEN TO CALL BACK (FIGURE 5.5)

You never want to be pushy with a client, but you also want to follow up. Here's the way we handle the situation.

FIFTEEN REASONS TO USE A SCRIPT (FIGURE 5.6)

Just in case you were wondering, here are the answers!

HOW TO DEVELOP YOUR OWN SCRIPT (FIGURE 5.7)

As we noted, scripts are very important, but if you don't know where to begin it can be difficult to write one. Just follow these 15 easy steps.

TARGET SCRIPT ORGANIZER (FIGURE 5.8)

This is a simple way to organize your script development.

RESPONSES TO ANTICIPATED OBJECTIONS (FIGURE 5.9)

More help in writing and organizing your script.

SCRIPTS (FIGURES 5.10–5.12)

Here are a few samples of the scripts that we use at the Sanford Group, Inc. Notice that we have a script to leave on an answering machine (this is free advertising!) and a follow-up letter for each call.

FIGURE 5.1

Words To Avoid/Words To Use

Avoid these words:

if	think	don't
maybe	perhaps	no
possibly	wondering	try
hope	can't	fail
sometimes	won't	attempt

Try to use a vocabulary that elicits a positive response in people.

- Use expressive, highly descriptive words:
  luxurious, beautiful, flawless

- Use dynamic words:
  powerful, energetic, impact, vigorous, cutting edge

- Use personal words:
  you, me, I, we, us, our

FIGURE 5.2

No, No Monotone

ENTHUS-I-A-S-M (*I Am S*old on *M*yself)!

- Sound awake and alive.

- Be interested in the person you are calling.

- Use a simple, down-to-earth script.

- Use simple, easy language.

- Don't use slang.

- Don't speak too fast or too loud.

- Sound relaxed.

- Pronounce your words carefully and do not run sentences together.

FIGURE 5.3

Control Your Environment

____ 1. Select a quiet environment free of distractions for calling.

____ 2. Have your desk free of distractions.

____ 3. Sit in a comfortable chair at a desk with good lighting.

____ 4. Eliminate all background noise.

____ 5. Do not allow *any* interruptions, under any circumstances.

____ 6. Place a small mirror in front of the phone so you can remember to smile.

____ 7. Use a headset.

____ 8. Stand up, move your hands and arms when you speak.

____ 9. Have your tally sheet readily available.

____ 10. Have your tickler cards ready.

____ 11. Look at goals hourly.

____ 12. Have good posture.

FIGURE 5.4

Five Qualities of a Good Telephone Voice

1. **Alertness**—Your voice should have sparkle and energy. Give the customer the impression that you are alive and wide awake. You must sound alert and anxious to be of help.

2. **Expressiveness**—You should vary your tone and rate of speech. You want to build a verbal picture with your voice.

3. **Distinctness**—Use clear articulation and enunciation. We tend to get lethargic in our day-to-day speech. Be careful not to drop the final consonant or breeze through the middle syllable. The telephone exaggerates this tendency, so let the sound come out clearly. When we are tired at the end of the day, we sometimes get lazy and slur our words.

4. **Conversational Tone**—You are a real human being talking with another real person. Be careful not to talk *at* the other person. Know the difference. Even when using a script, work hard to keep your tone conversational. Try to make your language simple and straightforward.

5. **Pleasantness**—Your voice should sound smooth and not jarring or whiny. Try to communicate with your voice that you are a pleasant and happy person. There is no room for shortness or anger. An "up" voice is much more appealing and compelling.

FIGURE 5.5

When To Call Back

People always ask, "How long should I wait before I call someone back after the first call?" Telemarketers do not want to cross the line of being "too pushy." There is no written rule. The best answer is the one the client or customer will give you.

Ask this question: "Mr. Reynolds, when do you think you will have a chance to review the information Walter Sanford sent you regarding the marketing of your home?" Always try to tie it to something they're going to do and let them give you the date. Be sure you mark a tickler card for the callback.

FIGURE 5.6

Fifteen Reasons To Use a Script

1. Provides security.

2. Provides reassurance on your direction.

3. Provides confidence.

4. Standardizes your techniques yielding a standard result.

5. Helps duplicate your success.

6. Maintains your focus.

7. Maintains your momentum.

8. Keeps you on track.

9. Gets more "yeses."

10. Helps overcome your resistance to calling.

11. Provides a way to measure results.

12. Provides a way to get the information to the prospect faster.

13. Makes the telemarketer sound very intelligent.

14. Gets the telemarketer to the next prospect faster.

15. Enables the prospect to understand the purpose of the call sooner.

FIGURE 5.7

How To Develop Your Own Script

1. Visualize the results you want to accomplish. The goal is to get an appointment.

2. Move backward from your goal and outline each major point.

3. Write a flowchart showing each step.

4. Think about open-ended questions to ask that will get the prospective client involved and interacting.

5. Write down in an outline how you will respond if they say "yes" and what you'll say if they say "no."

6. Imagine your prospects holding out their hands balanced as a scale. Provide them with so many benefits that the scale is tipped overwhelmingly in your favor for an appointment.

7. Since most people are visual thinkers, use visually descriptive words so they can picture the benefits.

8. Be clear and concise, personal and positive.

9. Work your outline through to a YES.

10. Write your outline into a completely detailed script.

11. Use your collective wisdom and compare your scripts.

12. Now reduce your script back down into a segmented outline.

13. Develop your segmented outline into a conversation.

14. Read it aloud several times to yourself and others to make sure it flows like a conversation.

15. Tape-record it, practice in the mirror, practice with others in the office. Never practice on the prospect.

FIGURE 5.8

Target Script Organizer

Script: _____ Date: _____

Describe the major goal of this script (reason for call).

_____

_____

_____

_____

List and describe any additional objectives.

_____

_____

_____

_____

Describe the agent and service being offered.

_____

_____

_____

_____

Describe the type(s) of prospect(s) being contacted (age, sex, location, etc.).

_____

_____

_____

_____

FIGURE 5.8 (Continued)

List the major benefits of REALTOR® and/or company.

_____

_____

_____

_____

List the benefits these features provide to the prospect.

_____

_____

_____

_____

What is the best reason for the prospect to act now?

_____

_____

_____

_____

Information to qualify the prospect:

_____

_____

_____

_____

FIGURE 5.9

Responses to Anticipated Objections

No interest:

_____

_____

_____

_____

_____

No authority to act:

_____

_____

_____

_____

_____

No need:

_____

_____

_____

_____

_____

No time:

_____

_____

_____

_____

_____

FIGURE 5.9 (Continued)

Previous bad experience:

_____

_____

_____

_____

_____

FIGURE 5.10

Assistant's People Farm

Script

Hi, this is [*assistant's name*]. I'm just calling to say hello and remind you I work for [*agent's name*], the top real estate agent/broker in [*city*]. [*Agent's name*] is really excited about 1993 and it's a great time to be buying real estate. Do you have any real estate plans for 1994?

YES—Great, have a great day and I'll have [*agent's name*] call you.

NO—Okay, great! If you do need a real estate agent at a later date, please remember me and [*agent's name*], the top agent in [*city*]. It was nice speaking with you and have a great day!

Answering Machine

Good (morning/afternoon/evening), this is [*assistant's name*] and I'm calling to say hello and remind you I work for the top real estate agent/broker in [*city*]. Please call me if you have any real estate questions or plans and I'll make sure [*agent's name*] gets the information. Thanks and have a great day!

Letter

[*Assistant's name*] is happy to announce that he/she has recently joined the real estate office of [*agent's name*]. [*Assistant's name*] will be assisting [*agent's name*], a top producer in the [*city*] area.

[*Assistant's name*] is a member of [*clubs/organizations*]. His/her wife/husband, [*spouse's name*], is employed by [*employment*] and they have [*#*] children, who attend [*schools*].

This new partnership will result in [*agent's name*] clients' properties being sold more efficiently, professionally and at top market value. Please call me at [*phone number*] if [*agent's name*] and I can be of any help to you with your real estate needs.

Sincerely,
[*assistant's name*]

FIGURE 5.11

FSBOs

Script

Hi, my name is [*assistant's name*]. I work for [*agent's name*], the leading real estate broker in [*city*].

I'm doing a quick survey of all the For Sale By Owners in the area to discover why they are trying to sell their homes themselves.

1. Why are you selling?

2. Where are you moving to?

3. How soon do you have to be there?

4. How long have you owned this property?

5. How did you determine your sales price?

6. What methods are you using to market your property?

7. Are you prepared to adjust your price down when working with a buyer?

8. Why did you decide to sell yourself rather than to list with a broker?

9. If you were to list, what would you expect that firm to do to get your home sold?

10. What is important about moving?

11. How is that important to you?

12. Ultimately, what will all of this do for you?

May I arrange an appointment for you to meet with [*agent's name*] so he/she can discuss his/her ideas on selling your property so you can [*achieve your highest value?*]?

FIGURE 5.11 (Continued)

YES: Great, would 7 o'clock or 8 o'clock tonight be more convenient for [*agent's name*] to speak with you?

NO: When can [*agent's name*] call you again for an appointment? Have you considered refinancing this property?

> **Yes:** I will have [*agent's name*]'s lender give you a call. Do you have any other property that you are thinking of selling?

> **No:** Let me ask you this. Which one of your friends, family or coworkers needs our help? Great! Thank you for your time, and when you think of real estate, call [*agent's name*].

Thanks, and have a great day!

Answering Machine

Good [morning/afternoon/evening], this is [*assistant's name*]. I'm calling for [*agent's name*], the top broker/agent in [*city*]. [*Agent's name*] has many successful marketing ideas, and he would love to speak with you at your convenience. Please call [*agent's name*] at [*phone number*]. Have a great day!

Letter

[*DATE*]

[*TITLE*] [*FIRST*] [*LAST*]
[*MAILING ADDRESS*]
[*CITY*], [*STATE*] [*ZIP*]

Dear [*SALUTATION*]:

I have embarked upon a unique way to assist people who are selling their own property. I have noticed that [*SUBJECT PROPERTY*] is one such property. I would like to offer you the following services:

- All the legal forms necessary to complete a sale in this paperwork-crazy world.

FIGURE 5.11 (Continued)

- Referrals to all the best escrow, title, insurance, property protection, property inspection, lending and termite companies.

- A telephone consultation with the top agent/broker in Long Beach.

- If you are relocating, a referral to the top agents in any city in the nation.

In return, I would appreciate the following:

- The names and phone numbers of buyers who do not buy your property.

- Referrals to any of your family, friends or coworkers who might be interested in buying and selling property in Long Beach and its adjacent cities.

- A referral of the people who need to list and sell their property in order to buy yours.

- Allow me to make a presentation of any marketing services should you consider listing your property.

I hope you appreciate this low-pressure attempt to do a little mutual "back scratching." I want to remain one of the top-producing brokers in the nation and will do whatever it takes to service your needs to this end. You may call my staff or me when you have a desire for any materials or services mentioned. Also, enclosed is a form to keep track of potential clientele for me.

Thank you in advance for what I think will be a profitable partnership.

Sincerely,

Walter S. Sanford
PRESIDENT/SGI

WSS: akm

FIGURE 5.12

Class "A" People Farm

Script

Good morning, this is [*assistant's name*], with [*agent's name*] office.

How are you today?

I am calling to find out if you have any real estate plans for 1993.

YES: Are you planning on moving/investing?
When do you plan on moving/investing?
Let me ask you this:
What is important about moving/investing?
How is that important to you?
Ultimately, what will all of this do for you?

NO: Okay, please remember us should any real estate needs arise.
Let me ask you this:
Which one of your friends, family or coworkers needs our help? Great!
Thank you for your time, and when you think of real estate, call [*agent's name*]!

Thank you for your time and have a great day!

Answering Machine

Good [morning/afternoon/evening], this is [*assistant's name*] with [*agent's name*], the leading real estate broker in [*city*]. [*Agent's name*] asked me to call and see if you have any plans for moving or investing at this time. Please call [*agent's name*] at [*phone number*]. Thank you and have a great day!

FIGURE 5.12 (Continued)

Letter

[DATE]

[TITLE] [FIRST] [LAST]
[MAILING ADDRESS]
[CITY], [STATE] [ZIP]

Dear [SALUTATION]:

I appreciated your taking the time to speak with me about our real estate market.

I have been fortunate to serve many happy clients, and it is my wish to someday be able to serve you. When the time comes that you need a competent real estate broker and adviser, remember Walter S. Sanford. Or, if you know of anyone who is thinking of purchasing or selling real estate, please give them my card.

I hope that if you have any further questions you will call me, or return the enclosed reply card at your convenience.

Most sincerely,

Walter S. Sanford
PRESIDENT/SGI

WSS: akm

P.S. Please keep this letter in your file for future reference.

6

The Importance
of Checklists

As you build your business, you'll need to have an assistant handling the details of listings and marketing, sales in progress and open houses. Checklists can help keep them on track. In this chapter we'll even show you how to avoid legal problems by keeping a conversation log.

When you fly on an airplane, the pilot and copilot always go through an extensive checklist. A pilot who has been flying for 20 years may be looking at the same checklist he has always used, but he still goes through each item on the list. A good real estate agent recognizes that checklists can be equally important for ensuring future success. If you forget an item that prevents a closing or causes great distress for a buyer or seller, it can be devastating to your career.

Every system that you use repeatedly should be in a checklist format. You are so busy, and real estate information can be so complicated, that you can't possibly remember every detail. Creating checklists for the things you do all the time will help prevent problems. If you have a checklist to refer to, it's a lot simpler than sitting there trying to remember what detail you have forgotten, and it will free up a lot of time for you.

What if your assistant goes on vacation or quits? If you have a detailed checklist, you will not be held hostage by this situation. You will be able to continue every project smoothly.

To develop a checklist:

1. Determine the subject.
2. List all steps, in detail and in order.
3. Include all pertinent information (phone numbers, addresses, reference file numbers).

4. Any piece of information that remains the same on each file should become a permanent part of the checklist (i.e., name, company, address, phone number of escrow, termite company, lender, etc.).

5. Compare your checklist with any others in existence to make sure you haven't forgotten any details or steps.

6. Work with your new checklist for one week and make any additions or corrections.

7. Review your checklist monthly to delete items that are not beneficial to you or your customers.

8. Consider any previous problems or experiences that you have encountered often, and make sure they are covered in your checklist.

LISTING AND MARKETING CHECKLIST (FIGURE 6.1)

This checklist is critical to following the marketing of a listing for the real estate agent. The list we use at the Sanford Group is very extensive. We change our checklist almost monthly, making additions, corrections and deletions. As one can see, we have included everything pertinent to the listing, from address to seller's name, information about brochures, tours, keys, open houses and lockboxes. Also included is information regarding the referral, referral fee and any referring clients. Look at our list and incorporate what fits your market; make your additions to monitor your listing; then work with your checklist for one week. Go back after the week and see what needs to be changed.

EXPIRED CHECKLIST (FIGURE 6.2)

When a listing expires and you do not extend it (unfortunately, those things *do* happen sometimes), it's important that you remember all the steps necessary to process the paperwork. How embarrassing it would be to receive a call two weeks after the listing expires and be asked to remove a sign and lockbox.

SALE IN PROCESS CHECKLIST (FIGURE 6.3)

This is the most important checklist for the real estate agent. You must monitor each step of a sale in process to ensure a successful close. We have included all pertinent information once again regarding the seller, buyer, all the affiliates involved and the financing. The checklist also includes tracking for various documents. Additionally, we have included at the close of escrow a thank-you letter reminder, "just sold" cards, and anniversary and closing statement letters. Remember, to personalize this for your market, just follow the same steps as in the Listing and Marketing Checklist.

COUNTDOWN TO CLOSE (FIGURE 6.4)

This form confirms all the dates necessary to achieve a smooth closing, and it's a way for you to verify the dates with your clients. We send this to the buyer's agent as well as the seller's agent.

OPEN HOUSE CHECKLIST (FIGURE 6.5)

There are so many things to remember prior to having an open house. Included are 40 items that will help you remember everything you need to accomplish by Sunday. This will save you from making flyers and trying to get an ad into the newspaper at the last minute on Friday afternoon.

OPEN HOUSE SURVEY (FIGURE 6.6)

This survey helps the hostess or agent to determine how that particular prospect found out about that house. We use this to determine if the newspaper, the flyer or the sign was the reason for their attendance, which is important for our cost/benefit analysis. We also use this survey to determine if the prospect is planning on buying or selling soon. Finally, the survey contains information we pass on to the seller regarding what the attendees liked and disliked about the property.

OPEN HOUSE OVER CHECKLIST (FIGURE 6.7)

When we conduct an open house, we have many things we must remember to complete prior to returning to the office. This list has everything from the signs and keys to the "thank you's."

CONVERSATION LOG (FIGURE 6.8)

It is important to document conversations of sellers or buyers. This form is placed in the listing file or the sale in process file. We document who, what, when, where and why.

BUYER CHECKLIST (FIGURE 6.9)

This is a step-by-step procedure of how we track a buyer we are working with. If for some reason the assistant who helps track the buyer is not available, the system is laid out so that anyone can take over.

BUYER PROFILE (FIGURE 6.10)

When we meet with a buyer, this is the information we obtain regarding price range and down payment. This form also logs appointments and phone calls.

BUYER SHOWING SCHEDULE (FIGURE 6.11)

This allows the agent to have proper showing instructions, keys and notes for all the properties that he or she will show that day. We also attach maps when necessary.

INSTRUCTIONS FOR BROCHURE CREATION (FIGURE 6.12)

Step-by-step procedures to create a property brochure are of great value to the agent. The agent can delegate this process to the assistant and never have to be concerned about the quality, brochure box or delivery.

FRONTLINE "PREFLIGHT" CHECKLIST (FIGURE 6.13)

No matter what size your office is, there are always certain duties that must be performed at the beginning of each day. Our checklist includes such items as turning off the alarm, distributing faxes, cutting out ads, watering plants and reviewing all messages.

CLOSING SEQUENCE (FIGURE 6.14)

How many times have you left the office and forgotten to turn off the coffee pot? How many times have you left the office and not locked all the doors? We have 14 items in our closing sequence. It will be simple for you to create your own.

FIGURE 6.1

Listing and Marketing Checklist 1993

Address: _____ MLS#: _____

Sq. Ft. from Tax: _____ Owner: _____ Measure: _____

Other: _____

Seller's Name: _____

(H) _____ (W) _____ FAX _____

Mail Address: _____

Name: _____

(H) _____ (W) _____ FAX _____

Mail Address: _____

Changes: Date: _____ Change: _____

Changes: Date: _____ Change: _____

Changes: Date: _____ Change: _____

Need from Seller: _____

_____

How: _____

Office Systems:

- Green Card two weeks before expiration date _____
- Trade Card _____
- New List Letter _____
- MLS faxed on _____
- Send detailed 11 _____
- Send BR Env   Y _____   N _____
- Permits   Y _____   N _____, Ordered _____
- Order CC&Rs   Y _____   N _____

FIGURE 6.1 (Continued)

- Order Termite   Now _____   Later _____
- Listing Distribution: Up Books _____
- Garage Inspect: Now _____   Later _____
- Follow-up Letter   1 _____   2 _____
- Expireds around New List _____
- Set Up Photo: Color _____   B/W _____

  Taken by & When _____

  Style: Regular _____   Heavy Paper/Color Photo _____

  Custom _____   Paper: White _____   Ivory _____

  Price: Y   N   Phone #:   Y   N

Distribution:

- Make 100 copies for caddy tray.
- Brochure Box: Yes _____   No _____
- Put 20 in brochure file.

Have: Area: _____   Type: _____

Telemarket: Who: _____   When: _____

Tours:

Belmont:	Order date _____	Tour date _____
	Letter sent _____	
Board:	Order date _____	Tour date _____
	Letter sent _____	
Bixby/NLB:	Order date _____	Tour date _____
	Letter sent _____	
Lakewood:	Order date _____	Tour date _____
	Letter sent _____	
Los Altos:	Order date _____	Tour date _____
	Letter sent _____	

FIGURE 6.1 (Continued)

Signs:

Post _____ Stake _____ Free _____

Custom _____ Free Commercial _____

Number of above:_____ Location(s): _____

Ordered: _____ By: _____

For Condos:

CC&Rs ordered and received? _____ HOA Phone #: _____

Total # of Units: _____ # Occupied: _____ # Rentals: _____

Currently for Sale: _____ Approx. $ in reserves: _____

Ordered financial statement/budget/bylaws from HOA on _____

Fieldwork:

Riders: 1. _____ 2. _____ 3. _____

4. _____ 5. _____

6. Special Order _____

Brochure Box: Y N Caddy Tray Y N Lockbox Guard Y N

Tent Card: Y N Sign Type Check Y N

Keys:

House _____ Gate _____ Mailbox _____ Garage _____

Multacc:
Y N Where: _____

Open House:

Promised: Y N

Open BA File:

Y N (Have Walter do BA checklist)

Source of Bus: _____

Referral Fees: _____

FIGURE 6.1 (Continued)

Referral Thank You and Agreement Letter: _____

Address & Phone # of Referring Client or Agent:

_____

_____

Extra Notes: _____

_____

_____

_____

FIGURE 6.2

Expired or Canceled Checklist

Conditional Release Form: _____

Mailed with SASE on: _____

Sent Release Letter: _____

Received back on: _____

Copy to File: _____

Registered Clients with Property Owner:

- _____

- _____

- _____

- _____

- _____

Change Card sent to Board: Yes _____ No _____
Date _____ By Whom _____

Sign ordered down: Yes _____ No _____
Date _____ By Whom _____

Riders (Lockbox/brochure box/caddy tray) picked up:
Yes _____ No _____
Date _____ By Whom _____

Keys returned: Yes _____ No _____
Date _____ By Whom _____

Thank You to Client: Yes _____ No _____
Sent _____ By Whom _____

Copy of Letter in File: Yes _____ No _____
Filed in LLB _____

Comments: _____
_____

FIGURE 6.3

Sale in Process Checklist 1993

Price: _____

Address of Sold Property: _____

MLS#: _____ Projected Closing Date: _____

	Sellers	**Buyers**

Name: _____ _____

_____ _____

Address: _____ _____

_____ _____

_____ _____

Phone: (H) _____ (H) _____

(W) _____ (W) _____

Agent Name: _____

Firm: _____

Address: _____

Phone: (W) _____ (H) _____

FAX _____ Mobile _____ Pager _____

Escrow
Name of Officer: Sue/Noreen
Company: Anchor Escrow
Address: 5602 E. Second Street, Long Beach, CA 90803
Phone: 434-4437 / Noreen's Direct # 434-3492
          Fax 439-2157

Escrow #: _____ Date of Opening: _____

FIGURE 6.3 (Continued)

Other Escrow

Name of Officer: _____

Company: _____

Address: _____

Phone: _____

Escrow # _____ Date of Opening: _____

Lender

Name of Firm:　PLAZA FUNDING FINANCIAL　　Agent:　JOHN BUSCH

Address:　800 S. Harbor Blvd., Ste 200, Anaheim
　　　　　　　Loan #: _____

Phone:　(W) 714-999-7722 X 630　　(FAX) 714-635-1030
　　　　　(PAGER) 714-324-7612

LENDER

Name of Firm: _____

Agent: _____ Broker: _____

Address: _____

Phone:　(W) _____ FAX _____ (H) _____

　　　　　Pager _____

Title Insurance

Name of Firm:　NORTH AMERICAN TITLE COMPANY
REP:　LYNN STEARNS
Phone:　(W) 988-7870　(Mobl) 500-8980　(FAX) 595-8104　(H) 433-1293

Short Rate: _____

Binder: _____
　　　　　　　　　　　(Notify Title Rep)

Other Title Insurance

Name of Firm: _____ Rep: _____

Phone:　(W) _____ FAX _____ (H) _____ Mobile _____

FIGURE 6.3 (Continued)

Notes: _____

_____

_____

_____

_____

Financing   **Commission**

Deposit _____   Gross _____

Add'l Deposit _____   Concessions _____

Balance Down _____   Referral Fee _____

1st _____   Net Commissions _____

2nd _____   Note Amount _____

3rd _____   Terms _____

Total Sales Price _____   Net Cash _____

Checklist

1. Deposit Receipt:
   To Client _____ Received from Client _____ File _____

2. Counteroffers:
   To Client _____ Received from Client _____ File _____

3. Counter to Counter:
   To Client _____ Received from Client _____ File _____

4. Escrow Instructions: File _____

5. Home Protection Plan: HAA   Member Broker: 24736

   (714) 978-0505 Ext. 200   Ordered _____

   NA _____   Confirmation # _____

6. Property Inspection: Bill Hogue (213) 985-3234
   Signature Inspection Services, 6268 Vista St., LB, CA

   Ordered _____   Appointment _____   Report in File _____

FIGURE 6.3 (Continued)

7. Permits: In File _____

   Ordered _____   NA _____   Receipted to Agent _____

8. In Escrow Letter: Seller _____

   Buyer _____

   Outside Affiliates: _____   _____   _____   _____

9. Seller Carryback Disclosure

   Buyer: Sent _____   Received _____

   Seller: Sent _____   Received _____

   Agent: Sent _____   Received _____

10. FIRPTA   Received from Seller _____

    Received from Agent _____

    File _____   To Agent _____

11. Listing Disclosure   To Buyer _____   Received _____

    To Seller _____   Received _____

    To Agent _____   Received _____

12. Agency Disclosure and   To Buyer _____   Received _____
    Confirmation
    To Seller _____   Received _____

    To Agent _____   Received _____

13. Environmental Hazard   To Buyer _____   Received _____
    Booklet
    To Seller _____   Received _____

    To Agent _____   Received _____

14. Earthquake Safety   To Buyer _____   Received _____

    To Seller _____   Received _____

    To Agent _____   Received _____

15. Sale Pending Rider Up _____

16. Caddy Tray/Brochures/Lockbox picked up (if applicable) _____

17. Homeowners Documents: Receipt to Agent _____

    Homeowners Association Name and Number _____

FIGURE 6.3 (Continued)

18. Up Book: In Escrow _____

19. Sale Board _____

20. Cash Flow Sheet _____

21. Termite: 1st Empire Termite Control, Phil Calia
        (310) 490-2188; Pager (714) 802-0693

    Other _____

    Limit _____   Access _____

    Ordered Inspection _____   Date of Work _____

    Sellers Notified _____   Sellers Notified _____

22. Garage Inspection: Date Ordered _____   NA _____

    Seller Notified _____   How Paid _____

    Appointment made for _____

23. Appraiser: _____

    Name and Address _____

    Works for _____   Appointment for _____

    Seller Notified _____   Time _____

    Who to meet Appraiser _____

    Appraiser _____

    Name and Address _____

    Works for _____   Appointment for _____

    Seller Notified _____   Time _____

    Who to meet Appraiser _____

24. Loan Approval _____   By Whom _____   Date _____

    Conditions: _____

25. Order Termite completion _____

26. Call sign down/get riders/lockbox/caddy tray _____

    _____

FIGURE 6.3 (Continued)

At Close of Escrow:

1. Report sold to MLS _____
2. Take out of up books _____
3. Thank-you letters to:
   - Client 1 _____
   - Client 2 _____
   - Client 3 _____
   - Other Broker _____
   - Lender _____
   - Other _____
4. "Just Sold" Cards (notify mail house) _____
5. Put in Anniversary Book _____
6. Sales to Date Ledger _____
7. People Farm/Red Dot/Have/Want (both sides of transaction) _____
8. Send sold info to *Press Telegram* "Real Estate Desk" _____
9. Closing statement and letter dated January 10th in file _____
10. Make Walter ask for referral _____
11. E&O Insurance Transaction Log _____
12. Closing statement & copy of check in file _____
13. Walter's office questionnaire sent to client _____
14. "Sprint" letter out to both sides of deal _____
15. Initial Closed File and convert to Sold File (file in garage) _____
16. Referral Fee Payments:

    Name _____

    Address _____

    Phone (B) _____ (H) _____

    Mobile _____ Beeper _____ FAX _____

    Amount $ _____ Date Sent _____

FIGURE 6.4

Countdown to Close

TO: John and Mary Minot
This letter is to confirm all the dates necessary to achieve a smooth closing. Please verify the dates with your clients and return a copy to me with your signature.

For Property at: 1734 Apple Way, Long Beach

	Goal Date	Actual Date
1. Contract acceptance with decision makers		
2. Property inspection by buyer		
3. Promissory Note inspection and approval		
4. Listing Disclosure signed		
5. Agency signed		
6. Service Contract approval		
7. Income/Expense approval		
8. Permit approval		
9. Inventory approval		
10. Escrow instructions prepared		
11. Escrow instructions signed		
12. Deposit submitted		
13. Deposit clears		
14. Professional property inspection		
15. Inspection accepted		
16. Estoppel Certificates approval		
17. Termite inspection		
18. Earthquake and Flood Zones		

FIGURE 6.4 (Continued)

	Goal Date	Actual Date
19. Deposit Increase to escrow		
20. Preliminary Title Report approval		
21. City approvals obtained		
22. Loan submitted complete to lender		
23. Appraisal made		
24. Appraisal done		
25. Termite work finished		
26. Obtain insurance		
27. Reappraisal done		
28. Other work finished		
29. PMI Approval		
30. FIRPTA signed		
31. Other contingencies cleared		
• _____		
• _____		
• _____		
32. Formal written loan approval		
33. Loan documents signed		
34. Cleared funds submitted for down payment		
35. Close of escrow		
36. Buyer's occupany		

Buyer's Agent _____

Date _____

Seller's Agent _____

Date _____

FIGURE 6.5

Open House Checklist

Date _____ **Date Completed** _____

Open House address: _____

____ 1. Notify owner, must be gone

____ 2. Sign or Open House Rider in yard

____ 3. *Press Telegram* advertising Saturday

____ 4. List to owners on preparing property

____ 5. Brochures ready

____ 6. Agent needed to assist—who:

____ 7. Bring radio

____ 8. Bring table and chair

____ 9. Key arrangement

____ 10. Special instructions:

____ 11. Open House invitation sent—quantity

Agent Preparation

____ 1. Brochures

____ 2. All flyers-combos

____ 3. Music

____ 4. Air freshener

____ 5. Deposit receipts

____ 6. Copy of listing

____ 7. Calculator

____ 8. Current Multiple

____ 9. Open House display cards

____ 10. Résumé

FIGURE 6.5 (Continued)

_____ 11. Flags at property line

_____ 12. Home Warranty information

_____ 13. Original plans available

_____ 14. Lighting

_____ 15. Scratch pads

_____ 16. Business cards

_____ 17. Guest cards

_____ 18. *Harmon Homes* magazine

_____ 19. Sample financing sheet

_____ 20. Clipboards (2)

_____ 21. Counteroffers

_____ 22. Buyers, Sellers net

_____ 23. Long Beach maps

_____ 24. Collect business cards

_____ 25. Put all valuables away

_____ 26. Flame logs

Cleanup

_____ 1. Leave explanation of day's activities

_____ 2. Leave cards at homes where I had signs up

FIGURE 6.6

Open House Survey

Name: _____

Address: _____ Home Phone: _____

City: _____ ZIP Code: _____ Bus. Phone: _____

How did you find out about this home?
Newspaper   Mailing   Sign   Other _____

Are you selling or planning to sell soon?   Yes   No

Are you currently buying or thinking about buying a property?   Yes   No

What did you like most about this property?

_____

What did you like least about this property?

_____

The sellers really appreciate your time and honesty in answering these questions. If I can ever help you in *any* real estate need, do not hesitate to contact me!

WALTER S. SANFORD/ *Long Beach's Leading Broker*

FIGURE 6.7

Open House Over Checklist

Seller: _____

Address: _____

Date: _____ Hostess: _____

____ 1. Open House signs (# _____)

____ 2. Complete checklist

____ 3. Note to owners, left/returned

____ 4. Key/lockbox key

____ 5. Cards/flyers returned/left

____ 6. Prospect follow-up cards/OH cards

____ 7. Open House Report completed

____ 8. Post hours worked _____ to _____

____ 9. Return sign ("Open Sunday 1–4")

____ 10. Send thank you to seller

____ 11. Send thank you to attendees

____ 12. Give Open House surveys to agent

FIGURE 6.8

Conversation Log

Who, what, when, where and why keeps the opposing attorney off the prowl!!!

Date all entries:

_____

_____

_____

_____

_____

_____

_____

_____

_____

_____

_____

_____

_____

_____

_____

FIGURE 6.9

Buyer Checklist

New Buyer Files

_____ 1. You will receive the Buyer Profile sheet from Walter or Monica out-lining the personal information and property parameters of a client. Double-hole-punch at the top and fasten in a letter-size file on the left-hand side.

_____ 2. Enter the client's personal and property information in program 91 on BOLTS. You will get a printout of all properties meeting those parameters. Double-hole-punch the printout at the top and fasten on the right-hand side of the file.

_____ 3. Run 11s (detailed listing information) on each of the properties on the printout. Cut the 11s just below the showing instruction area (so you will cut off the listing office and agent information).

_____ 4. Type a mailing label for the client and stick it on a 6 × 9 mailing envelope. Include in the envelope on the first mailing:
(1) Property printouts enclosed card all 11s
(1) REALTOR® map with Walter's card
(1) List of Abbreviations packet

Sending Out Buyer Info

These are the supplies that should be provided for you before you begin:

    1 stack computer printouts on white paper
    1 stack preaddressed envelopes
    1 stack brown card inserts to enclose with printouts

Always cut just above the first line that begins MLS NO. _For the bottom:_ Always cut just above the line that reads "L/O #." (If you are careful here, you will not cut off the previous line beginning two-thirds of the way across the page with the word "SHOW.") You may throw away the lines of each printout that you cut off and also the list of MLS numbers where I have identified each client's printouts. I have marked these areas with green highlighter on the first page.

For printouts that are not complete on one page, do not cut off the blank white part at the bottom of the page on which the printout begins. On the next page, where the printout continues, cut JUST ABOVE THE FIRST LINE THAT

FIGURE 6.9 (Continued)

APPEARS, no matter which line of the printout it is. Cut the bottom of the printout at the regular spot, just above the part that starts with "L/O #." Tape the bottom part of the printout to the top part JUST UNDER THE LAST LINE ON THE TOP PART. See the printout in Minnie Mouse's envelope for an example. I have also marked the first one for you. Please remove the yellow Post-Its before putting in the envelope. Printouts that are crossed out may be thrown away. DO NOT SEND. These did not meet the criteria of the buyer. When you have completed cutting all the printouts for one person, stack them neatly together (they should all be about the same size) and put one of the brown cards on top. Now put the printouts with brown card on top in the envelope so that they face the back of the envelope (the part that you will seal).

You are done with one buyer! CONGRATULATIONS!! Proceed with the other buyers until all are complete.

Buyer File

_____ 1. Send appointment letter and enter client into people farm; make copy to put into their file. Confirm appointment by phone on the day of appointment.

_____ 2. Put together file on client to include
- manila folder with name on tab.
- two-page buyer worksheet.
- buyer profile worksheet.
- two sheets of property comparison forms.
- Walter's credentials.
- propaganda or handouts regarding buying property.
- a map.
- copy of appointment letter.
- Up Call card original given from Walter.

_____ 3. Place folder in BA file drawer.

BB File

_____ 1. Once a "Buyer A" client has been taken out of active use, use their file with all information kept in BB files in garage.

_____ 2. People farm card is updated at the time of transfer of file to garage.

FIGURE 6.9 (Continued)

Schedule Appointments

_____ 1. Run Program 11 on all property that is to be shown.

_____ 2. Call the listing office to verify that the property is still available. If it is, ask for showing instructions, and make note if a key is to be picked up from the office.

_____ 3. Cross off list if property is PENDING SALE or SOLD.

_____ 4. Make a copy of a map of the area of properties to be shown.

_____ 5. Mark the exact location of the properties with an "X" and circle it.

_____ 6. Call the owners or tenants and tell them the day and time the property is to be shown. (Verify if there is a lockbox and its location).

_____ 7. Schedule properties that are located near each other to be shown within the same time frame—within 15- to 30-minute intervals.

_____ 8. After appointments have been confirmed, mark the computer printout with the time to be shown and the order number in which each is to be shown.

_____ 9. Make a list of all properties to be shown in order and then mark on the map the corresponding number of the property.

_____ 10. Make a photocopy of the printouts for the buyer's file.

_____ 11. Return everything to Walter's or Monica's desk for showing.

FIGURE 6.10

Buyer Profile

Date: _____

Name: _____

Address: _____

Phones: (H) _____ (W) _____ (F) _____

Geographical Area(s): _____

_____

Type: _____   Price Range: _____

Type: _____   Price Range: _____

Type: _____   Price Range: _____

Size Requirements: _____

Down: $ _____   Type Financing: _____

Special Features to Include: _____

_____

Special Features to Exclude: _____

Appointments/Mailings/Phone Calls:

1. _____   4. _____

2. _____   5. _____

3. _____   6. _____

Instructions to:

1. Send current inventory   _____

2. Put and keep on daily/weekly watch   _____

3. Set up BA file for Monica   _____

4. Put Wants in BOLTS   _____

FIGURE 6.10 (Continued)

5. Run Haves through SGI computer and
   give to telemarketer   _____

6. If not a BA, where does this Paper go?   _____

7. Fax needs to top agents   _____

8. Have information given to   Lender Name _____
   (for prequalification)

9. PF/cred/card/mag card   _____

FIGURE 6.11

Buyer Showing Schedule

Date of Showing: _____

First Showing Time: _____

Buyers: _____

Map Attached _____   11s Attached _____

Attached	Showing Time	Property Address/Instructions/Notes
_____	_____	_____
		Show: _____
		Keys: _____
		Notes: _____
_____	_____	_____
		Show: _____
		Keys: _____
		Notes: _____
_____	_____	_____
		Show: _____
		Keys: _____
		Notes: _____
_____	_____	_____
		Show: _____
		Keys: _____
		Notes: _____

FIGURE 6.11 (Continued)

Attached	Showing Time	Property Address/Instructions/Notes
_____	_____	_____
		Show: _____
		Keys: _____
		Notes: _____

FIGURE 6.12

Instructions for Brochure Creation

Seller Name: _____

Date: _____

Prepared by: _____

1. Use camera in closet to take picture and develop at MOTO PHOTO.

2. Attach the picture to the designated area. Make sure that the picture fits inside the outline of the box. If not, cut off white edges of the black and white picture and then place in the box. **Note:** It is better to have the picture too small in the outline box area rather than overlapping the outline.

3. Photocopy the master copy of the brochure in the file labeled "Master Copies."

4. Keep the master copy of the brochure in the "Master Copies" file.

5. Make sure that you go through all brochures once a week to see if you have pictures and enough copies in your file, and remake new brochures for the sign person to take out every Saturday.

6. If you are unsure what brochures are needed, either ask the creator of the brochure or the sign person if they need any more brochures to refill the box.

7. Brochures for brochure boxes consist of a brochure, "How Walter S. Sanford Can Assist You to Buy This Property" sheet, and a business reply card stapled together in size order in the left-hand corner.

8. Make ten copies for the Seller.

9. Make ten copies for the listing file (middle section).

10. Make ten copies for the brochure file in the office.

11. Make 30 copies for a caddy tray.

12. Make 30 copies for brochure box.

13. Make one copy for the upbook.

14. Place this form in the listing file.

15. Call Title Rep to deliver new flyers to all real estate companies.

FIGURE 6.13

Frontline "Preflight" Checklist

The cooperation of the frontline person is necessary in completing the following duties and providing a wonderful environment for our clients and staff. Assisting in the marketing of our properties is why we are here!

_____ 1. Turn off alarm.

_____ 2. Turn on most common-area lights.

_____ 3. Open all blinds.

_____ 4. Turn off the back outside light.

_____ 5. Turn on photocopy machine and make sure all paper bins are full.

_____ 6. Check all toner in every machine; make sure they are full.

_____ 7. Distribute all facsimile transmissions to the person who is receiving.

_____ 8. Take the "on hold ad" tape player off of "pause."

_____ 9. Take the phone off of night mode.

_____ 10. Retrieve all messages from the recorder and distribute them.

_____ 11. Go through all message books on all desks for hidden messages and distribute them.

_____ 12. On Monday morning retrieve all advertising (_Press Telegram_, Termite Publications, Grunion, etc.). Write addresses on them, put them in plastic sheets and keep in front of the Up books. Two months of ads are to be kept.

_____ 13. • Run a bulletin (Program 34) and lay on Walter's desk daily.
        • Run a one-line list of all office listings (Program 12) and put in front of the Up book weekly.

_____ 14. Make sure welcoming board is filled out with the names of Walter's appointments for that day.

_____ 15. Make sure the following areas are presentable to clients:
        • Reception desk and area cleaned
        • Conference room desk and area cleaned

FIGURE 6.13 (Continued)

_____ 16. On _Tuesdays:_ After the Belmont tour is finished, call Century 21 Coastline (310-439-2161) and ask the secretary for the price/averages of all the properties we had on tour that day, then give Walter all information in writing.

_____ 17. **Hotsheets:** Have Jim, the field coordinator, take them down to Office Club to print, collate and staple 300 copies. They must be given to Walter prior to Tuesday morning on the weeks that Walter goes to the Board Breakfast.

_____ 18. This instruction sheet is to be kept in the front of both Up books.

_____ 19. Pull a Program 11 after MLS Book comes out on all of your new listings and send a copy of MLS Book page and copy of Program 11 to client with insert. Check accuracy against the original listing file.

_____ 20. Water all plants and flowers inside building, whether temporary or permanent, every other day.

_____ 21. Every other Tuesday, check that there is $35 in petty cash to pay the cleaning lady.

_____ 22. All buyers go to Monica, then Walter, in that order.

_____ 23. Agent calls go to Tori or Walter, in that order.

_____ 24. Personal calls go to the designated person. These are the lowest priority. Excessive personal calls are forbidden and cannot happen in this office.

_____ 25. Rental calls go to Tori. If she is not in:
- Information/location request—answer their questions!
- Wants to see—follow showing instructions or give to Tori.

_____ 26. Newsletter phone calls go to Monica or Margaret, in this order. Use order form and be sure to take a good message.

_____ 27. On miscellaneous phone calls, write down who the call was for and what it was regarding. Be specific, please!

FIGURE 6.14

Closing Sequence

The last one out and the last one at the mentioned/affected station is to complete the following:

_____ 1. Turn copier off.

_____ 2. Turn coffee off.

_____ 3. Close out postal machine.

_____ 4. Turn all lights off.

_____ 5. Reception area cleaned in and out.

_____ 6. Conference room cleaned.

_____ 7. All mail taken and mailed.

_____ 8. Computers and typewriters turned off.

_____ 9. Answer machine on.

_____ 10. All exit doors locked.

_____ 11. Turn off air conditioner or heater.

_____ 12. Put "on hold" on pause.

_____ 13. Close all blinds.

_____ 14. Command One into alarm.

7

Delegation Makes
Things Happen

While traveling throughout North America giving seminars on working with assistants, I have discovered that many real estate agents cannot delegate effectively. The main reason seems to be that they do not want to relinquish control. Some real estate agents are afraid to allow anyone to assist them out of fear that the client will not be treated properly or the paperwork will not be done according to their standards.

Another reason real estate agents do not delegate effectively is that they do not take the time to give clear and concise instructions. Real estate agents are salespeople and not teachers. Therefore, they may not be able to properly communicate *how* to do something. Instead they say, "Oh, never mind. By the time I tell you how to do it, I can do it myself." However, this is a fallacy. In all likelihood, that task never gets done.

A terrific agent in the Dallas–Fort Worth area told me that she had over 700 Christmas cards that were addressed, stamped and sealed—all lying under her desk. Unfortunately, it was March and they had never been mailed. The reason she did not mail them was that she did not like her assistant's handwriting; it did not meet her standards. She not only was frustrated but had lost money, too! She focused on the method—not the results.

Most real estate agents fail to realize that you must focus on results in order to reach the next level of income and production.

In this chapter we will go into why you should delegate, how to effectively delegate and ways to break each task into steps so that it is done properly. Guidelines are offered on what sort of tasks to delegate and how to start doing so. A worksheet is also here to help you decide whom to delegate to. Additionally, there are steps to prioritizing, ways to save time and over 500 items to delegate.

Delegation can give you the gift of time, allow you to multiply yourself and help you go to the next income level. And it can do all of this while reducing your stress. In fact, you'll have the time to bring more creative thinking to your work. When considering delegation, also look for tasks that can be eliminated entirely. In fact, this is the largest benefit that delegating offers—finding chores that no one needs to do.

Passing a job on to other people generally helps to motivate them and allows them to develop new capabilities. Sometimes an assistant can do certain things faster than the agent can!

Prospecting is one of the most important items your assistant can do. Have him or her spend one hour a day calling your past clients, expired listings or FSBOs. Also have your assistant make you more productive by confirming all your listing appointments and sending out a packet that sells you very strongly. You'll want to include testimonials from satisfied customers and addresses of transactions that you (or your company) have done in the area.

Also market to owners of non-owner-occupied homes, which you can get from title companies. And don't forget your past clients; send them letters on each anniversary of their home purchase. You don't have the time to contact these people, but your assistant does. Out-of-area brokers are another group it pays to contact, and fax your own best listings to the top agents in your area.

You'll become more productive by teaching your assistant to qualify buyers over the phone. You can even delegate tasks to buyers! Give them a list of homes for sale and a map, and ask them to drive by those properties. Afterward they can tell you which ones they want to look at. Send them new listings each week. Your assistant thus can keep numerous buyers tied to you, while you are spending little or no time on them.

Holding open houses, monitoring supplies, submitting press releases, doing mailings to your farms, managing your income properties, reconciling your checkbook, monitoring cash flow to make sure that closings and expenses will match, calling sellers every ten days and processing listings are all things your assistant can do for you.

As needed, you can hire others—such as a field coordinator—to put up lockboxes, brochure boxes and sign riders; make bank deposits; purchase supplies; deliver listing packages, gifts and messages; and provide personal assistance, such as going to the laundry for you.

NINE REASONS TO DELEGATE

1. Delegation can relieve you of certain tasks, giving you the gift of time to learn and grow.

2. Delegation gives you the power to multiply yourself many times over by using the time, knowledge, experience and creative power of other people to supplement your own.
3. Delegation fosters team building by developing in others a sense of belonging, importance and success.
4. Delegation encourages creativity, initiative and independence for you and for those to whom you choose to delegate.
5. Delegation offers opportunity for growth and the development of new skills.
6. Delegation inspires motivation, as others feel their opinions count and their input matters.
7. Delegation boosts productivity and shows others how their efforts contribute to the whole.
8. Delegation develops better decision-making skills for both you and those to whom you have chosen to delegate.
9. Delegation empowers others to create, and people support what they help create.

TWENTY-SIX DELEGATION HINTS

Here are some hints on what and how you can delegate.

1. Delegate the whole, if possible, not just part of a larger task, to provide the other with a full sense of accomplishment.
2. Delegate routine tasks, even if you think you could do them more quickly yourself.
3. *Train,* if necessary. It will save you time in the long run.
4. Be willing to share your knowledge and skills.
5. Build in *flexibility.* A safety net here is to cross-train. It is best if more than one or two people can complete a task.
6. Specify in detail what you want accomplished. *Indicate what steps need to be taken.* If the task is large, break it into manageable parts for the person to whom you are delegating.
7. Communicate how the delegated task *fits into the overall project or goal.*
8. Specify the *scope and limits of the responsibilities and authority* for the person to whom you are delegating. Should he or she make decisions or consult with and defer to you?
9. Do not solve problems for the person to whom you are delegating. *Have the person propose solutions.* Then help choose the best solution.
10. *Establish firm time lines.* But do include a time cushion in case the project takes longer than expected.
11. Establish *agreed-upon checkpoints and monitor progress.*
12. Focus on *results, not methods.*

13. *Give feedback.* The purpose of giving feedback is to reinforce desirable behavior and discourage undesirable behavior. It is most powerful if given immediately following the behavior.
14. Give those to whom you have delegated *full credit* for their accomplishments and ideas.
15. Be willing to *relinquish some authority, control and responsibility.*
16. Delegate details that take the biggest amount of your time.
17. Delegate the job that you are least qualified to do.
18. Delegate all tasks that someone else could do. Know the specialties of those on your team.
19. Delegate tasks in which 80–90 percent efficiency is acceptable.
20. Prepare yourself. Have a firm grasp of your overall goals. List your tasks and responsibilities in this order:
    • Tasks I must do personally
    • Tasks others can do
    • Tasks that can be simplified
    • Tasks that can be eliminated
21. Make a plan for each of these. See Tasks Worksheet (Figure 7.1).
22. Analyze the abilities of those you could designate to do the task. What are their talents, strengths and weaknesses? How do these people fit into the big picture—into the household, the group, the committee or the corporation? Use a chart to help you with this. See Delegation Worksheet (Figure 7.3).
23. Be available.
24. Keep communication lines open. Be an active listener.
25. Evaluate.
26. Be a nonperfectionist!

Remember: before delegating, consider whether the task could be simplified or eliminated. The following forms will make delegation easier. You should refer also to some of the planning forms shown in chapter 3, so that what you delegate will fit in with the assistant's daily activities and overall goals.

TASK WORKSHEET (FIGURE 7.1)

This worksheet is an example of how you should divide tasks into four categories.

Task Worksheet (Figure 7.2)

This is a blank worksheet like 7.1 above for your use.

DELEGATION WORKSHEET (FIGURE 7.3)

This worksheet is an example of the steps to delegate. This will allow you to monitor each step.

Delegation Worksheet (Figure 7.4)

This is a blank copy of form 7.3 for your use.

TODAY'S PRIORITIES (FIGURE 7.5)

Actually itemizing the tasks you need to do, placing them in order of priority, then checking them off when you are done makes the job easier.

HELP WANTED (FIGURE 7.6)

This checklist will help you start thinking about and formulating the jobs you can delegate to an assistant. The following responsibilities can be accomplished by one or more people daily, weekly or monthly. Put a check mark by the ones that would be of most benefit to you. I would then suggest including them in a written job description for your assistant.

SIXTEEN WAYS TO SAVE TIME AS AN ASSISTANT (FIGURE 7.7)

This is just a few ways to better manage your assistant's time.

TEN GOLDEN RULES OF REAL ESTATE TIME MANAGEMENT (FIGURE 7.8)

Review this often to make sure that you are not creating more problems for yourself.

FIGURE 7.1

Sample Task Worksheet

Tasks I must do personally:
   Call John Nieman.
   Make dentist appointment.
   Call sellers at Beauty Bay.
   Call Jane at IBM for new lead.

Tasks others can do:
   Expired letters out
   Escrow update
   Accounts balanced
   Listing showing update
   Car washed

Tasks that could be simplified:
   Review checklist on listing for duplications.
   Put lockbox on at time of signing of listing.
   Enter all expenses/check numbers in computer.

Tasks that could be eliminated:
   Eliminate gifts at closing.
   Eliminate delivery of property brochures; have title rep deliver or we
      mail.
   Eliminate office supply expenditures; have supplies donated by
      affiliates.

After listing your tasks in the proper categories above, take immediate action to eliminate unnecessary jobs. Then concentrate your attention on the tasks that can be simplified and those that can be delegated. Make a specific plan for these. Now review the tasks that you must do personally, and consider that these should be the most important elements of your job and should fill the major portion of your time.

FIGURE 7.2

Task Worksheet

Tasks I must do personally:
Tasks others can do:
Tasks that could be simplified:
Tasks that could be eliminated:

After listing your tasks in the proper categories above, take immediate action to eliminate unnecessary jobs. Then concentrate your attention on the tasks that can be simplified and those that can be delegated. Make a specific plan for these. Now review the tasks that you must do personally, and consider that these should be the most important elements of your job and should fill the major portion of your time.

FIGURE 7.3

Sample Delegation Worksheet

Task	Who could handle it?	What skills, talents, training, knowledge does this person have?
Holiday calling	All assistants and affiliates	Role playing several times with Walter and Monica Computer skills
What preparation does he/she need? script mirror call log names/phone numbers enthusiasm	**What are his/her current time constraints?** One hour a day from November to January is the commitment.	**How will the delegated task be monitored?** Monica will collect and monitor call logs each day.

Quality of results:

FIGURE 7.4

Delegation Worksheet

Task	Who could handle it?	What skills, talents, training, knowledge does this person have?
What preparation does he/she need?	**What are his/her current time constraints?**	**How will the delegated task be monitored?**
Quality of results:		

FIGURE 7.5

Today's Priorities

Date _____ / _____

	Priority:	Done:	List:
1.			
2.			
3.			
4.			
5.			
6.			
7.			
8.			
9.			
10.			
11.			
12.			
13.			
14.			
15.			
16.			
17.			
18.			

FIGURE 7.6

Help Wanted

- Return all phone calls of the agent within a three-hour period.
- Always use formal salutations.
- Answer all phone calls by the second ring.
- Use agreed-upon greeting for answering the phone.
- Use an energetic and enthusiastic voice on the phone.
- Prepare all listing packages.
- Confirm all listing appointments for agent.
- Order owner and encumbrance reports from title company.
- Maintain listing file.
- Produce and update all listing checklists.
- Prepare weekly office reports.
- Update expired listings daily.
- Research all expireds.
- Call all expireds.
- Maintain past expired files.
- Maintain expired watch.
- Prepare special expired package for special delivery.
- Deliver special expired package.
- Send thank-you letter to seller after listing signed.
- Track showings of listings for agent.
- Call seller with results of showings.
- Visit every new listing.
- Personally or by phone, introduce yourself to the seller.
- Inform agent of listings with no showings.
- Send thank-you notes to all appointments daily.

FIGURE 7.6 (Continued)

- Obtain information from assessor's office.
- Prepare all Comparative Market Analyses.
- Process all listings to MLS.
- Handle all listing changes to MLS (price, addendum changes).
- Prepare property brochure.
- Distribute property brochure to seller.
- Distribute property brochure to agents/offices in city.
- Provide information to appraisers.
- Enter data on computer for all listings.
- Enter data regarding pendings, solds and changes.
- Run agent reports daily regarding new listings/solds.
- Handle all agent expired listings.
- Handle all agent extensions of current listings.
- Process all contracts.
- Order all title work.
- Prepare closing statements.
- Maintain closing checklist.
- Handle all communications with the escrow company.
- Meet with all affiliates.
- Meet with lenders, escrow, termite and title to develop a team.
- Handle all title company communications regarding the closings.
- Handle all lender communications.
- Attend closings for the agent.
- Complete weekly under contract and closed reports.
- Maintain monthly financial status reports.
- Maintain cash-flow chart.
- Handle all correspondence.

FIGURE 7.6 (Continued)

- Open all mail and sort for agent.
- Maintain buyer communications.
- Set up showing appointments.
- Call on showings by other agents.
- Enter all showings in the computer for tracking.
- Run showing reports for agent.
- Watch solds that affect agent's listings.
- Report properties for the office tour.
- Set up appointment with seller for office tour.
- Report and post sold/just listed on office scoreboard.
- Set weekly goals.
- Maintain and monitor weekly goals.
- Finalize sold files of closings.
- Send thank you after closing letters to affiliates.
- Send thank you after closing letter to other agent.
- Send thank you after closing letter to seller/buyer.
- Enter anniversary date of closing in computer.
- Generate closing statement/letter dated Jan. 10.
- Maintain sale-in-process/closing checklist.
- Send out In Escrow letter upon opening sale in process.
- Communicate with lender regarding sale.
- Handle all incoming calls.
- Screen all incoming calls.
- Floor calls: obtain all information before giving out information.
- Use the Buyer Questionnaire.
- Use the Seller Questionnaire.
- Prepare any and all legal forms.

FIGURE 7.6 (Continued)

- Prepare APOD (Annual Property Operating Data).
- Schedule all real estate appointments.
- Schedule all personal appointments for the agent.
- Handle all travel arrangements for the agent.
- Use the travel checklist.
- Prepare travel information for the agent.
- Put up signs.
- Make keys for properties.
- Maintain key board.
- Measure properties for agent.
- Do personal errands when needed for agent.
- Handle all thank-yous for agent.
- Schedule Year at a Glance for agent and assistant.
- Maintain Day Timer for agent.
- Record all information in Day Timer regarding anniversaries, birthdays and appointments.
- Record all prospecting time for agent in planner.
- Record all vacation times for agent and assistant well in advance.
- Update all personal financial statements yearly for agent.
- Update résumé.
- Prepare year-end statistical reports (referrals from past clients and customers, number of listings sold, number of other broker sold, etc.).
- Balance personal checking accounts.
- Mail out newsletters.
- Mail to agent's people farm four times a year.
- Call agent's people farm four times a year.
- Do holiday calling.
- Prepare profit and loss statements for accountant.

FIGURE 7.6 (Continued)

- Maintain tax records for accountant.
- Maintain expense/income records.
- Mail out July Fourth firecracker mailer.
- Deliver client Christmas presents.
- Preview each listing after listings have been received; ring doorbell, introduce yourself; if not home, leave card.
- Cut out all newspaper advertising of agent's listings.
- Send advertising monthly to sellers.
- Save all personal promotion ads of agents in file.
- Write all ads.
- Place all ads.
- Use a Dictaphone.
- Use a microcassette recorder.
- Update sellers weekly/every two weeks.
- Attend all weekly sales meetings.
- Attend all marketing meetings.
- Ensure timely completion of all correspondence.
- Have daily communication meeting with agent.
- Fill out daily communication log.
- Create a letter file in computer of frequently used letters.
- Systematize all letters.
- Maintain letters to co-op agents/buyers/sellers/affiliates.
- Take care of gifts to lenders, title company, etc.
- Keep track of all inventory.
- Order all supplies.
- Have affiliates contribute to supplies.
- Keep updated pictures on file for the agent.
- Order stationery, cards and brochures.

FIGURE 7.6 (Continued)

- Maintain and order promotional items.
- Send expired letters.
- Send anniversary letters each day.
- Send closing letter/statement on Jan. 10.
- Handle all vendors.
- Help agent with taking car to get washed/gas/maintenance.
- Order Christmas cards in July.
- Organize move-in box for new buyers.
- Purchase supplies for move-in box.
- Send congratulations to "Just Engaged."
- Send congratulations to "Just Married."
- Prospect and call (Just Engaged and Just Married).
- Organize mass mailings.
- Organize all bulk mailings.
- Personally meet with all affiliates.
- Order your own business cards.
- Mail your own business card with every bill.
- Pay agent's monthly bills.
- Set up a FSBO program.
- Mail letters to FSBOs.
- Personally deliver FSBO package.
- Call FSBOs for agent and make appointments.
- Purchase all stamps and mailing supplies.
- Install For Sale signs.
- Install Sold signs.
- Pick up all signs.
- Handle registrations for all educational seminars and events.

FIGURE 7.6 (Continued)

- Send out press releases.
- Write two press releases each month.
- Personally meet the real estate editor of your local publications.
- Submit and follow up on all press releases.
- Research city and county records for non-owner-occupied homes.
- Mail to non-owner-occupieds.
- Follow up with non-owner-occupieds with a letter or call.
- Review all closing documents.
- Fax all new listings to top agents in your local board.
- Fax information for the agent.
- Handle all photocopying for the agent.
- Take dictation.
- Send flowers or gifts on the agent's behalf.
- Track rental expenses on rental properties for agent.
- Serve as a contact for renters of agent's property.
- Make all bank deposits for agent.
- Make all rent deposits for agent.
- Maintain rental deposit savings account.
- Track all pending sales.
- Update current mailing lists.
- Maintain current mailing lists.
- Update personal marketing book.
- Write and place all home magazine classified ads.
- Schedule Open House with sellers.
- Write ad for Open House.
- Submit ad to newspaper for Open House.
- Get signs ready for Open House.

FIGURE 7.6 (Continued)

- Put signs out for Open House.
- Prepare all flyers for the Open House.
- Put Open House flyers out for the neighborhood.
- Write Open House notes to neighbors.
- Serve as host/hostess for Open House.
- Write thank-you note to seller.
- Write thank-you notes to attendees of Open House.
- Distribute flyers to other agents.
- Maintain Open House checklist.
- Hold Open Houses for agents.
- Coordinate with seller for REALTOR® open house.
- Coordinate with board for REALTOR® open house.
- Send REALTOR® evaluation forms.
- Send copies of all ads to owners.
- Order sign up.
- Order sign down.
- Prepare buyer file.
- Make showing appointments for agent.
- Make map for showings for agent if necessary.
- Get all keys ready for agent.
- Send buyers weekly updates on all new listings.
- Maintain investment records.
- Pay insurance policies.
- Maintain all insurance records for agent.
- Monitor work for the second assistant.
- Direct and delegate work to the second assistant.
- Handle all commission status reports.

FIGURE 7.6 (Continued)

- Maintain year-to-date production status reports.

- Track vacant homes.

- Become an income generator.

- Maintain office accounts.

- Record all calls.

- Organize agent's desk and surrounding areas.

- Maintain agent's files.

- Mail out to investors in Long Beach.

- Update job description.

- Create an office policy manual.

- Create an office procedures manual.

- Update policy and procedures manual quarterly.

- Call past clients for referrals for agent.

- Determine ways to decrease expenses (monthly).

- Determine ways to increase business/leads (monthly).

- Determine ways to save time (monthly).

- Evaluate all checklists for efficiency.

- Bring a personal referral to agent once a month.

- Develop an assistant people farm of your sphere of influence.

- Keep master copies of all important documents.

- Read all pertinent real estate periodicals, magazines, etc., to help agent with new cutting-edge ideas.

- Listen to all real estate educational tapes to further your real estate expertise.

- Attend all seminars that will further your skills as a real estate assistant.

- Create a "Clients for Life" system.

- Keep agent on track for goals and production.

- Knock on doors and distribute information regarding the agent and property in the neighborhood.

FIGURE 7.7

Sixteen Ways To Save Time
as an Assistant

1. Bunch all phone calls and return them all at once rather than intermittently during the day.

2. Place all photocopying in a file and do it all at once so that you aren't going to the photocopying machine every hour.

3. Have a three-tiered wire basket file on your desk. The first level is Top Priority; the second level is Do Today; and the third level is Do Sometime. This will prevent the agent from throwing files all over your desk and make him or her prioritize their importance for you.

4. Have one hour of silence during the day. Assistants all over America tell me that if they had one hour of uninterrupted time, they would get an entire day's worth of work done. So, I suggest you have your receptionist tell people this when they call between 10 and 11 AM: "I'm sorry, Monica is not available at this time; she is in conference. Please give me a detailed message. She can call you back between 11 and 11:30, or tell me what time is best for you."

   If you have voice mail, use this message: "Good morning, this is Monica. Your call is very important to me. I am in the office and I'm in conference. Please leave me a detailed message and I will call you back with the information between 11 and 11:30. Have a great day, and I look forward to speaking with you."

5. Before you leave each night, spend the last five minutes writing down the top priorities of the next day. This will get you on track right away in the morning. Also list any possible questions you might have for the agent.

6. Before you leave for the day, always make sure your desk is neat. A cluttered desk full of piles will depress you as you walk into the office.

7. Use a color file to hold all your reading material. When you are placed on hold, you can also be doing something productive.

8. Use a microcassette recorder. This will allow you to record important reminders and also organize any special projects. The agent can use this for letters, reminders and listing information to you.

9. Speak to the agent about constant interruptions. Try having the agent log his or her questions until there are at least five, and then interrupt you. Constant agent interruptions are a costly management problem.

FIGURE 7.7 (Continued)

10. Always meet standing up.

11. Meet with the agent once a day. This need not be a prearranged time, but maybe when the agent gets to the office it can be done immediately.

12. Honesty will save you lots of time.

13. Always get right to the point: "How can I help you?"

14. Pay all bills at the same time, once a month. Also, keep all bills to be paid in the same area, file or box.

15. Call on the escrows/sale-in-process transactions at the same time every week. Have the loan processor and escrow agents ready for your call by prearranging the time.

16. When someone comes uninvited into your office or work space, stand up and walk them toward the door as you answer their question.

FIGURE 7.8

Ten Golden Rules of
Real Estate Time Management

1. Understand the value of your time and all that you must accomplish each day.
    *   Yesterday is a canceled check.
    *   Tomorrow is a promissory note.
    *   Today is cash; spend those minutes wisely.

2. Set priorities on a daily basis as well as a long-term basis.

3. Set both short-term and long-term goals.

4. Make a "To Do" list every day.

5. Budget your time and stick to your schedule.

6. Be flexible when you need to.

7. Learn to say no.

8. Use a planning system.

9. Don't be a perfectionist—nobody will like you and you won't like yourself.

10. Get help.

8

The Assistant as a
Profit Center

Although just saving you time and helping make your office run more smoothly is a benefit that helps your profits, it's even better if your assistant actually brings in business. Check your state laws to see what someone who does not have a real estate license can and can't do.

We pay bonuses to assistants if Walter gets a listing appointment as a result of their calls to expired listings, FSBOs and their personal spheres of influence. We also use a buyer survey form to get all the information on potential purchasers who call. By finding out buyers' motivation and resources upfront, Walter can tell whether it's worthwhile to call them back. A bonus is given to the assistant who took the completed form after the buyer closes on a home purchase. A similar form is provided to use with sellers, to find out if a caller has a genuine interest in selling.

In this chapter we also describe "The Irreplaceable Employee" to provide assistants with an ideal. Assistants also can learn "Twenty Ways to Pay for Yourself," a list of tasks they can do to bring in revenue.

Sharing your goals is important in order to build a team. Goals need to be set in terms of listings, listing presentations, deals in escrow, deals closed, FSBOs contacted, expireds contacted, people farm contacted, past clients contacted and buyers worked with.

You'll also discover that assistants can come up with the best ways to reduce costs. For instance, if you have paper that has been used on just one side, turn it over for in-office photocopies or scratch paper. In a big office this can save a few trees as well as several thousand dollars a year.

One of our assistants suggested that Walter ask the title company to contribute for the hamburgers and hot dogs at a barbecue for her condo building.

Walter had never sold a unit there before. But we got a good response for a free barbecue by poolside, where people could come to meet Walter and chat with their neighbors. Walter got two listings, and the assistant who suggested the barbecue met her future husband there! But the point is to multiply yourself by getting your assistant to prospect for you with his or her friends and relatives. Get others to help you as well. For instance, have the termite company remove the sign and lockbox from a sold home.

Delegating, using checklists and focusing on profits has helped us streamline and become very productive. One assistant in our office can handle over 150 listings and more than 30 escrows, plus oversee 90 income units—and show buyers around! And don't forget to regularly ask them for a money-saving idea, a money-making idea, a time-saving idea and a referral.

We have developed a system that allows most agents to easily afford an assistant. An assistant is NOT a liability. No longer do we see the real estate assistant as a paper pusher and message taker. An assistant is an income-producing and lead-generating team player. Your assistant will free you to speak with buyers and sellers and negotiate contracts. Everything else should be delegated to the assistant.

With the effective use of an assistant, agents can dominate their markets and make incredible incomes. Superstars of the real estate industry generally have one to ten assistants. High production can only come from a partnership between the agent and an assistant.

Ways of strengthening that working relationship are included in this chapter. For example, we have quarterly "meet our goal" bonuses, which might be a gift certificate or a lunch and movie outing. Finding out what motivates your assistant is important in getting the performance you are looking for.

WHAT DO I SAY? (BUYERS; FIGURE 8.1)

This form helps the assistant handle the incoming buyer call correctly when the agent is not available. If the form is filled out correctly and it leads to an appointment, which leads to a sale, then a bonus is due the assistant.

WHAT DO I SAY? (SELLERS; FIGURE 8.2)

This form is like 8.1 but pertains to sellers. The assistant can effectively handle all incoming seller calls and then turn the lead over to the agent.

TWENTY WAYS TO INCREASE INCOME (FIGURE 8.3)

This form is given to the assistant as a reminder of the importance of being a profit center. It shows how an assistant can generate income and help to decrease expenses.

THE IRREPLACEABLE EMPLOYEE (FIGURE 8.4)

We do not keep this information a secret! I share it with you in hopes that the learning curve to becoming irreplaceable is shortened.

RESPONSIBILITIES OF THE AGENT (FIGURE 8.5)

These 14 points will establish a plan to keep the agent on track as a boss.

RESPONSIBILITIES OF THE ASSISTANT (FIGURE 8.6)

These 15 points will keep the assistant on track as a top-performing real estate assistant.

FIGURE 8.1

WHAT DO I SAY?

(Buyers)
The $100-at-Close Magic Questions

Date: _____ Phone: (H) _____ (W) _____

Buyers' Names: _____

Address: _____

1. How long have you been looking? _____

2. Are you working with another agent or broker? _____

   If yes, who? _____

3. How many are in your family? _____

4. Do you own now, or are you renting? _____

5. Must you sell before buying (or complete the lease period before buying)?

   _____ If yes, how long? _____

6. Have you seen any homes or investment properties that you really liked?

   _____

7. If yes, why didn't you buy it? _____

8. How soon do you need to move? _____

9. If we can find the right property, are you prepared to make a decision at

   that time? _____

10. What price range have you been considering? $ _____

11. How much cash do you want to use for the purchase? $ _____

12. Do you have a budget for monthly payments? _____

13. How many bedrooms? _____ Sq. Ft.? _____ Units? _____

14. Do you prefer a particular location in the city? _____

15. Is there anyone else who will be helping you make the decision about

    buying? _____

FIGURE 8.1 (Continued)

16. Do you have any special requirements for your new property? _____

_____

17. Where are you employed? _____

18. Where is your spouse employed? _____

19. If Walter gives you 100 percent of his time, will you buy your new property from him? _____

20. What times are best for you to look? _____

21. I will have Walter call you so that he can go over details of purchase. What is the best time to have him call you? _____

Summary:

Price Range: $_____ to $_____

Down Payment: $_____ to $_____

Bdrms/Baths _____/_____ Units _____ to _____ Sq. Ft. _____

Locations: _____

Comments: _____

_____

FIGURE 8.2

WHAT DO I SAY?

(Sellers)
The $100-at-Close Magic Questions

Property: _____

Date: _____ Operator: _____

Sellers' Names: _____

Mailing Address: _____

Phone: (H) _____ (W) _____

(H) _____ (W) _____

1. How did you hear of Walter Sanford? _____
_____

2. Why do you want to sell? _____

3. Referred by: (Name) _____

(Address) _____

(Phone) _____

Referral Fee: _____

4. When would it be convenient for all decision makers to be present and meet with Walter?

_____ _____
(Day)   (Date)

_____ at _____ or Sanford Group
(Time)   (Address)   (Preferred)

5. How many people will present? _____

6. Do you own any other properties in the area? _____

If yes, where? _____

FIGURE 8.2 (Continued)

7. Are you thinking of listing them also? _____

8. Where are you moving to? _____

9. Do you know a real estate professional there? _____

_____

10. When do you need to sell? _____

11. How much do you want to list for? _____

12. How much are your underlying loans? 1st $ _____

                                                                 2nd $ _____

                                                                 3rd $ _____

13. Do you need a 1031 Tax Deferred Exchange? _____

14. Who else are you interviewing? When?

Agent	Office	Appointment Date/Time
_____	_____	_____
_____	_____	_____
_____	_____	_____

Remember, Walter wants to be the seller's last appointment. Make this possible and reschedule if necessary. You can say, "Meeting with all of the other brokers first will guarantee a maximum of questions. Walter can better serve you if you have the maximum amount of questions available."

15. If Walter answers all of your questions to your satisfaction, will you list

your property when you meet Walter? _____

16. What criteria are you going to use in hiring an agent?

_____

_____

FIGURE 8.2 (Continued)

17. **Property Matrix:**

Type	Sq. Ft.	Bed/Bath	Income	Length of Lease

18. Other Amenities of Property: _____

_____

19. To: _____

Top Priority TODAY	Fast TODAY/TOM.	Standard TOMORROW	Low Priority LATER

20. Parameters:

Area(s) _____ Type _____ Size _____

Area(s) _____ Type _____ Size _____

N/ _____ S/ _____ E/ _____ W/ _____

(Low) $ _____ (High) $ _____

21. Number of Clients/Copies _____

22. Walter's follow-up instructions:

____ • Run an 11 check of the presentation property.

____ • Check to see if sellers own any other property in areas close to Long Beach and inform Walter.
Address (es):

_____

_____

____ • Run Walter's list for listing presentation.

____ • Please confirm that all decision makers will be present at meeting.

____ • Deliver confirmation package to them.

FIGURE 8.2 (Continued)

_____ • Add to people farm.

_____ • Input Haves/Wants.

_____ • Order Super/Regular Property Profile.

_____ • Is CMA Complete/Accurate?

_____ • Confirm that presentation is complete.

_____ • Initial.

FIGURE 8.3

Twenty Ways To Increase Income Through Assistants

1. Goal each month: Bring one buyer or seller to agent from assistant's people farm.

2. Goal each month: Bring one money-saving idea to end-of-month meeting.

3. Goal each month: Bring one money-making idea to end-of-month meeting.

4. Goal each month: Bring one time-saving idea to end-of-month meeting.

5. Have a press release published at least once a week.

6. Cut down on office supplies; ask affiliates to provide.

7. Shield agent from unnecessary calls so that he or she can list and sell.

8. Keep agent off personal time-waster calls.

9. Help agent be accountable to goals each month.

10. Keep agent on track each day!

11. Always be positive for agent, which will help keep the agent positive.

12. Telemarket past clients for business one hour a day.

13. Telemarket expireds or drop off expired packages.

14. Return phone calls of top priority.

15. Learn to prescreen buyer calls.

16. Learn to screen possible seller calls.

17. Develop an excellent memory for sellers and addresses, important clients, etc.

18. Hold open houses; be a host/hostess.

19. Everywhere you go, promote your agent!

20. Pass out your card everywhere, and build your database!

FIGURE 8.4

The Irreplaceable Employee

1. Ask not what your boss can do for you, but what you can do for your boss!
2. Make the agent's problems your own.
3. Win without intimidation; be nice.
4. Don't lead a company revolt—walk away from negativism.
5. Don't panic, don't be afraid; ask for help.
6. Be smart but not too smart. Make your boss feel smarter.
7. Know how and when to present ideas; timing is everything.
8. Don't take it personally; develop thick skin.
9. Be a "can-do" person.
10. Take it one task at a time.
11. Ask for more challenges and work.
12. It's the responsibility of the assistant to ask, "What is the deadline?" Then meet the deadline.
13. Take work home occasionally. It demonstrates that you are a true team player.
14. Know the two ways to come to work: on time or early.
15. Occasionally, eat lunch at your desk.
16. Occasionally, stay until the job is done.
17. Cooperate with the office.
18. Know your boss, his or her personality and moods.
19. Let your boss know the work you're doing.
20. Read, listen to tapes and watch videos on real estate. Tell your agent about any new ideas that might make a difference in your business.
21. Watch expenses.
22. Don't waste supplies.
23. Cultivate client relationships.

FIGURE 8.4 (Continued)

24. Sell your agent.

25. Be effective in communications.

26. Look good.

27. Take the peer test; compare yourself.

28. Turn problems around—be creative, inventive.

29. Talk to your family about your job.

30. Have a positive attitude.

31. Be organized.

32. Take pride.

33. Care.

34. Go the extra mile.

35. Put the agent first.

36. Lighten up!

37. Listen, pay attention and follow directions.

38. Be a team player.

39. Be discreet.

40. Bring referrals to the agent!

FIGURE 8.5

Responsibilities of the Agent

1. Give the assistant all the information needed to answer questions and handle minor problems.

2. Delegate a matching amount of authority with each responsibility.

3. If you leave the office, keep the assistant informed of your whereabouts, where you can be reached and when you will return.

4. Keep paperwork moving. Don't delay in reviewing drafts or making decisions.

5. Avoid perfectionism. Strive for excellence, because excellence equals results.

6. Use a dictating machine. It is five times faster than writing by hand.

7. Authorize your assistant to answer correspondence as his or her ability and experience permit.

8. Discipline yourself to avoid interrupting your secretary unnecessarily. Jot down five items to be discussed later if immediate answers are not essential.

9. Establish a plan for controlling telephone and drop-in visitors.

10. Avoid asking your secretary to bring you coffee and do personal errands. If he or she is truly a member of your management team, he or she will volunteer on occasion in order to conserve your time.

11. At regular intervals, review performance, discuss mutual problems and reinforce the team relationship. A meeting every three months for this purpose is a good guideline to follow.

12. Take the time to train the assistant to make independent decisions.

13. Empower the secretary to be a miniexecutive—your personal representative.

14. Recognize and reward—Recognize and reward—

FIGURE 8.6

Responsibilities of the Real Estate Assistant

1. Know the boss's short-term and long-term goals.

2. Develop your job description with a manual of office operating procedures.

3. Take the initiative. Don't wait to be told to do a job. Handle minor problems and learn which should be referred to the boss.

4. Confer with the agent on how to handle phone calls and screen calls and visitors.

5. Have a written plan for each day.

6. Prepare your plan at the end of the day for the next day.

7. Organize your desk at the end of the day.

8. Keep a written list of all tasks requested by the agent.

9. Don't waste the agent's time. Be prepared for stand-up meetings, with necessary papers and questions at hand.

10. Let the agent know what your needs are in order to do a good job.

11. Be positive.

12. Work hard to make your agent look good. Winners always take their support team with them when they move up the ladder.

13. Communicate, communicate, communicate! Ask for assistance, be honest and professional, and be sensitive to the pressures and responsibilities of your boss.

14. Recognize the agent as a risk taker.

15. Maintain a good sense of humor.

Glossary

ad call Abbreviation for advertising call; most common in newspaper ad.

ALTA title policy Type of title insurance policy issued by title insurance companies that expands the risks normally insured against under standard policies to include unrecorded mechanic's liens; unrecorded physical easements; facts a physical survey would show; water and mineral rights; and right of parties in possession, such as tenants and buyers under unrecorded instruments.

acceptance When the seller or agent's principal agrees to the terms of the sale, approves the negotiation on the part of the agent and acknowledges receipt of the deposit in subscribing to the agreement of sale.

agent One who represents another from whom he or she has derived authority.

appraisal Estimate and opinion of value; a conclusion resulting from the analysis of facts.

assessed value Value placed on property as a basis for taxation.

assessment Valuation of property for the purpose of levying a tax, or the amount of the tax levied.

assignment Transfer to another of the whole of any property, real or personal, in possession or in action, or of any estate or right therein.

assignor One who assigns or transfers property.

assigns, assignees Those to whom property shall have been transferred.

assumption of mortgage The taking of title to property by a grantee who thereupon assumes liability for payment of an existing note secured by a mortgage or deed of trust against the property; becoming a coguarantor for the payment of a mortgage or deed of trust note.

balloon payment Final installment on a note that is greater than the preceding installment payments and that pays the note in full.

beneficiary (1) One who is entitled to the benefit of a trust; (2) one who receives profit from an estate, the title of which is vested in a trustee; (3) the lender on the security of a note and deed of trust.

broker A person employed by another for a fee to carry on any of the activities listed in the license law definition of broker.

CC&Rs Abbreviation for covenants, conditions and restrictions.

capitalization rate Rate of interest that is considered a reasonable return on the investment and that is used in the process of determining value based upon net income. Also, the yield rate that is necessary to attract the average investor to a particular kind of investment. This amortization factor can be determined in various ways—for example, by the straight-line depreciation method. (To explore this subject in greater depth, refer to current real estate appraisal texts.)

close for appointment   Asking a property owner for a definite appointment to make a listing presentation.

closing   Use of various techniques to gain agreement.

closing statement   Accounting of funds made separately to both buyer and seller (required by law to be made at the completion of every real estate transaction).

condominium   Unit in a multifamily structure that combines individual fee ownership with joint ownership of common areas of the structure and the land.

counteroffer   Contract to purchase from a seller to a buyer, usually written on a separate contract in response to a contract offer from a buyer.

CMA   Abbreviation for the Competitive Market Analysis.

comparable property   Home similar in location, size, improvements, condition, price, etc.

compare   The process of equating the subject property to homes recently sold, homes currently for sale and homes that did not sell (expired).

competitive market analysis   A form to display properties recently sold, properties for sale and expired properties.

comps   Real estate slang word for comparable properties.

contract   Binding agreement, either written or oral, to do or not to do certain things.

Documentary Transfer Tax   State enabling act allowing a county to tax all transfers of real property located in the county. Notice of payment is entered on face of the deed or on a separate paper filed with the deed.

earnest money   Down payment made by a purchaser of real estate as evidence of good faith.

effective interest   Percentage of interest actually being paid by a borrower for use of money.

encumbrance   Anything that affects or limits the fee-simple title to property, such as mortgages, easements or restrictions of any kind. Liens are special encumbrances that make the property security for the payment of a debt or obligation, such as mortgages and taxes.

escrow   The deposit of instruments and funds with instructions to a neutral party to carry out the provisions of an agreement or contract; when everything is deposited to enable carrying out the instructions, it is called a complete or perfect escrow.

ethics   Principles of conduct, justness and fairness that address the duties an individual or member of a profession owes to the public, to clients or patrons and to other professionals.

expired listing   A property listed for sale that has not sold and for which the listing contract has run out.

farming A systematic campaign for contacting property owners on a routine basis.

first mortgage Legal document pledging collateral for a loan (see "mortgage") that has first priority over all other claims against a property except taxes and bonded indebtedness.

first trust deed Legal document pledging collateral for a loan (see "trust deed") that has first priority over all other claims against the property except taxes and bonded indebtedness.

FSBO For Sale By Owner.

grant Technical term made use of in deeds of conveyance of lands transfer.

grant deed Deed in which *grant* is used as the word of conveyance. The grantor implies warranty that he or she has not already conveyed to any other person, and that the property conveyed is free from encumbrances of the grantor or any person claiming under him or her, including taxes, assessments and other liens.

grantee The purchaser; a person to whom a grant is made.

grantor Seller of property; one who signs a deed.

installment note Note that provides for payments of a certain sum or amount on specified dates.

joint tenancy Joint ownership by two or more persons with right of survivorship; all joint tenants own equal interest and have equal rights in the property.

legal description A description recognized by law; a description by which property can be located by reference to government surveys or approved recorded maps.

lis pendens Suit pending, usually recorded so as to give notice of pending litigation.

listing An employment contract between principal and agent authorizing the agent to perform services for the principal involving the latter's property; listing contracts are entered into for the purpose of securing persons to buy, lease or rent property. Employment of an agent by a prospective purchaser or lessee to locate property for purchase or lease may be considered a listing.

listing presentation A preplanned presentation delivered to a property owner for the purpose of obtaining a listing.

loan application Information on which the lender decides whether to make the loan. The application defines the terms of the loan contract; lists the applicant's name, place of employment, salary, bank accounts and credit references; and describes the real estate that is to be mortgaged. It also stipulates the amount being applied for and repayment terms.

loan closing When all conditions have been met, the loan officer authorizes the recording of the trust deed or mortgage. The disbursement procedure of funds is similar to the closing of real estate sales escrow. The borrower can expect to receive less than the amount of the loan, as title, recording, service and other fees may be withheld, or he or she can expect to deposit the cost of these items into the loan escrow. This process is sometimes called "funding" the loan.

market price   The price paid regardless of pressures, motives or intelligence.

mortgagee   One to whom a mortgagor gives a mortgage to secure a loan or performance of an obligation; a lender.

mortgagor   One who gives a mortgage on his or her property to secure a loan or assure performance of an obligation; a borrower.

Multiple Listing   A listing, usually an exclusive right to sell, taken by a member of an organization composed of real estate brokers, with the provision that all members will have the opportunity to find an interested client; a cooperative listing.

net sheet   A form that shows the normal cost of selling property. It shows the approximate net proceeds after all costs are subtracted.

offer   Contract to purchase from a buyer to a seller.

party wall   Wall erected on the line between two adjoining properties, which are under different ownership, for the use of both properties.

personal property   Any property that is not real property.

power of attorney   Instrument authorizing a person to act as the agent of the person granting it, and a general power authorizing the agent to act generally on behalf of the principal. A special power limits the agent to a particular act—for example, a landowner may grant an agent special power of attorney to convey a single, specific parcel of property. Under the provisions of a general power of attorney, the agent having the power may convey any or all property of the principal granting the general power of attorney.

principal   (1) The employer of an agent; (2) the amount of money borrowed.

principal note   Promissory note that is secured by a mortgage or trust deed.

promissory note   Following a loan commitment from a lender, the borrower signs this document, promising to repay the loan under stipulated terms. The promissory note establishes personal liability for its repayment.

proration of taxes   Division of taxes equally or proportionately based upon use.

prospecting   Contacting people for the purpose of finding someone who wants to sell or buy.

qualifying   A procedure to determine if a buyer is ready, willing and able to buy.

quitclaim deed   Document that relinquishes any interest in property that the grantor may have.

real estate board   An organization whose members consist primarily of real estate brokers and salespeople.

REALTOR®   A real estate broker or salesperson holding active membership in a real estate board affiliated with the National Association of REALTORS®.

recapture   Rate of interest necessary to provide for the return of an investment. Not to be confused with interest rate, which is a rate of interest on an investment.

reconveyance Transfer of land title from one person to the immediate preceding owner. This particular instrument of transfer is commonly used when the performance or debt is satisfied under the terms of a deed of trust, and the trustee conveys the title that was being held on condition back to the owner.

recording The process of placing a document on file with a designated public official, which makes it a matter of public record. This public official is usually known as the county recorder. The recorder confirms the fact that a document has been given to him or her by stamping it and indicating the time of day and the date when it was officially placed on file.

showing Abbreviation for showing a buyer property.

sign call Call made to an office whose sign has been placed on a property.

tenancy in common Ownership by two or more persons who hold undivided interest without right of survivorship; interests need not be equal.

title Instrument that proves legal ownership of land.

title insurance Insurance written by a title company to protect a property owner against loss if title is imperfect.

title report A report, made by a title company before issuing title insurance, that discloses condition of the title.

trust account An account, separate and physically segregated from broker's own funds, in which broker is required by law to deposit all funds collected for clients.

trust deed Just as with a mortgage, this is a legal document by which a borrower pledges certain real property or collateral as guarantee for the repayment of a loan. There is the third, neutral party (just as there is with an escrow) who receives the trust deed, who is called the trustee. And, finally, there is the lender, who is called the beneficiary, because the lender benefits from the pledge arrangement: In the event of a default, the trustee can sell the property and transfer the money from the sale to the lender as payment of the debt.

trustee One who holds property in trust for another to secure the performance of an obligation.

trustor One who deeds property to a trustee to be held as security until the trustor has performed any obligations to a lender under terms of a deed trust.

underwriting Technical analysis by a lender to determine a borrower's ability to repay a contemplated loan.

warranty deed A document used to convey real property that contains warranties of title and quiet possession; the grantor thus agrees to defend the premises against the lawful claims of third persons. It is commonly used in many states, but in others the grant deed has supplanted it due to the modern practice of securing title insurance policies, which have reduced the importance of express and implied warranty in deeds.

wraparound mortgage Second mortgage that enables the borrower to add to development without refinancing the first mortgage at substantially higher current rates.

yield Interest earned by an investor on his or her investment (or by a bank on the money it has lent). Also called return.

zone Area set off by the proper authorities for specific use; subject to certain restrictions or restraints.

zoning Act of city or county authorities specifying type of use to which property may be put in specific areas.

Index

SYSTEMS AND SEMINARS FOR CAREER-ORIENTED REAL ESTATE AGENTS AND ASSISTANTS

Although Monica Reynolds still manages Walter Sanford's extremely busy real estate business, she believes it is important to share the proven systems and profit-building methods that she has developed. Monica has trained more than 3,000 assistants throughout North America and has helped numerous agents to realize the goal of obtaining the perfect assistant. A series of tapes are available to augment the information in this manual, as well as a variety of other systems to help both the agent and the assistant achieve their goals. Monica is also available for speaking at individual seminars, sales rallies or conventions. Please contact Kimberly Hawkins at 1-800-7-WALTER for further information.